Spirituality And Recovery

Spirituality And Recovery

A Guide To Positive Living

by
Father Leo Booth

Revised Edition

Health Communications, Inc.
Deerfield Beach, Florida

Published by:
Health Communications, Inc.
Enterprise Center
3201 S.W. 15th Street
Deerfield Beach, FL 33442

ISBN 0-932194-28-1

A Special Dedication To
Mother and Father

Other Books by
Father Leo Booth

Say Yes To Life . . . Daily Meditations for Recovery
Meditations For Compulsive People . . . God in the Odd

Acknowledgments

In order to "Walk on Water", it is helpful to be surrounded by special people who, by their love, support and practical criticisms, enable the journey of life to be made; in the writing of this book, I have specifically appreciated the following people:

The Reverend Carroll C. Barbour — a special friend, brother priest, gifted teacher and confidant.

Bishop Colin Docker — the man who took a risk with my "moment" and gave me a new ministry.

James Fulton — a personal friend and Administrator in Chemical Dependency, who saw that special "spark" of Spirituality in treatment.

Dr. Conway and Charlotte Hunter — dear friends who share the dream and generously help create the vision.

Barbara McRae — a friend and secretary whose loyalty enables freedom.

Dr. William Rader — an insightful thinker and searcher who provoked thought and stimulated my determinism.

Bishop Robert Rusack — a Bishop who loves through his ready support and practiced detachment.

Pat Ryder — who practically created this book with hours of typing, correction and struggle with the author's bad handwriting.

Charles Siron — a friend for all seasons.

A special mention must be made of Gloria Coker who, with little
   guidelines from the author, created such wonderful sketches.
And numerous colleagues and friends who, in the dropping of a
   word, created a story line.

                                                    Thank You.

Table Of Contents

Introduction

This revised edition of *Spirituality And Recovery* attempts to explain the important distinction between spirituality and religion, making the essential point that spirituality is a gift bestowed on all human beings, regardless of creed, class, color or sexual orientation. Spirituality is recognizing that we have the power to change. We have the power to develop the healing process. Spirituality is recovery.

In this revised edition, I also have sought to relate spirituality to some of the key concerns facing recovering people today: relationships, relapse and treatment issues. You should not need to be a philosopher, theologian or student of medieval history to understand the living challenge that spirituality offers, so I have sought to relate spirituality to contemporary and everyday situations. God is to be found in the dust.

I believe the all-embracing message that spirituality brings is essential to the living of a positive lifestyle. It is too important to be missed. May you discover it now in the living of your life.

Fr. Leo

WALKING ON WATER

To walk on water is to experience the joy in living. Know the laugh and human embrace as well as the tear. Walking on water is seeing and feeling the given miracle of life in every moment. It is the shouted "yes" to all that life will bring.

Life is but a series of patterned moments, and with every moment comes decision. Which way shall I go? What shall I do? Shall I say, "Yes" or "no?" Our comfortableness with these decisions affect whether we live life or simply endure it.

Participate or Spectate.

Shape or Wait.

God gives us the gift of life, and then invites us to create
through it,
with it,
in it.

In this sense, we are divine. In this sense, we are part of the Divine Drama. Every religion, creed and culture gives this message, but few people listen. We miss the most important message in life: "YOU ARE TERRIFIC".

We walk on water when we hear and accept this message.

The idea for the title of this book comes from an incident that is recorded about Jesus and His disciples. In St. Matthew's Gospel we read:

After sending the people away, he went up a hill by himself to pray. When evening came, Jesus was there alone; and by this time the boat was far out in the lake, tossed about by the waves, because the wind was blowing against it.

Between three and six o'clock in the morning, Jesus came to the disciples, walking on the water. When they saw him walking on the water, they were terrified. "It's a ghost!" they said, and screamed with fear.

Jesus spoke to them at once. "Courage!" he said. "It is I. Don't be afraid!"

Then Peter spoke up. "Lord, if it is really you, order me to come out on the water to you."

"Come!" answered Jesus. So Peter got out of the boat and started walking on the water to Jesus. But when he noticed the strong wind, he was afraid and started to sink down in the water. "Save me, Lord!" he cried. [1]

This incident tells more than Jesus doing supernatural feats on a stormy sea, with Peter trying to imitate. The miracle is in the words, "take courage". Relative to the physical and emotional needs of mankind, walking on water means nothing. The incident only astounds and amazes people. But the creative insight comes when we absorb the revealed courage into our own lives. When we take the courage that Peter reveals and relate it to our personal needs in our times.

When we attempt to live on our own, away from those who have always supported and rescued us from life.

When we try to pass the examination this year.

When we, although blind or infirm, continue to seek for employment.

The miracle is in adapting the "take courage" into our own lives.

We are the miracle. WE ARE TERRIFIC.

Every area of life can reveal this truth. In personal relationships,
music,
religion,
theatre,
politics,
humor,
craftsmanship,
suffering,
poetry.

It is all out there, if only we have the eyes to see.

I recognized this when I was reading about the defection to the West of the famous ballet dancer, Rudolf Nureyev.

On May 11, 1961, Rudolf Nureyev flew from Leningrad with the Kirov Ballet Company to dance in Paris. To the Russian authorities, Nureyev had already proven himself to be an individualist and a rebel. Not surprisingly, they had concerns about his even being in the West. They decided to send a telegram to Paris, demanding that he return to Moscow, supposedly to perform before the Kremlin. Instead, Nureyev placed himself into the hands of the French police, and asked for protection. Seizing the opportunity of the moment, he chose to defect. In the defection was the courage . . . chose to leave his family and country . . . chose to leave the Kirov Ballet Company for . . . ? At the time he did not know what.

Nureyev was taken by the police and placed in a solitary room. He says, "Then there was silence. I was alone. Four white walls and two doors. Two exits to two different lives."²

On that seemingly ordinary day in Le Bourget Airport in Paris, Rudolf Nureyev took courage, and decided to shape his destiny. In the moment of defection, his muted yesterdays generated a choice.

"For me this was already a return to dignity—the right to choose, the right I cherish most of all, that of self-determination."

The balanced life of Spirituality is reached when we comfortably can hold together opposites. Freedom and dependence. Seeking God's will in the doing of our own. Trusting and waiting on Him, and yet exercising that divine gift of self-determination. Holding together forces that often seem to point in opposite directions.

Paradoxes of God.

Paradoxes of being human.

Paradoxes of life.

It all begins to make sense when we accept that God wills for us real freedom. He created us to make choices. He created us to create. The dignity and nobility that all human beings can achieve is dependent upon this real freedom. In this gift is the miracle. We are human beings—not puppets on a string.

Our dependence upon God speaks of our creativeness. We did not create this universe. We are part of the miracle we call life. And yet, part of the reality of this miracle is that we have the responsibility of decision. God's will for us is seeing our creative abilities and choosing to cooperate in positive living.

God is the continuous positive energy.
The Love for the world.
He invites us to be involved. That makes us terrific!
To stand around and wait for God to make decisions in our lives is to miss the point. That is apathy or cowardice or stupidity. God has already made a timeless decision. He wants what is best for us. He also wants us to want it.

The human paradox and confusion is revealed in these further remarks made by Nureyev. "I did not have courage to stay here— just to come and stay. I did not have courage . . . I remember I went to Church, I went to Mary . . . and I said, 'Make it so that I stay without me doing it, you know, let it happen . . . without me doing it . . . that it will happen, . . . arrange so that I will stay.' "

We all know these feelings.

I know the fear of making a mistake, making the wrong decision. The desire to have others make the decision. Others make the choice. Others make it happen. Sometimes God.

I believe God makes good things happen in the world by putting deep within all of us the potential ingredients for good. As Genesis says in the creation account, "And it was good." We have the capacity for great goodness. The "catch of freedom" comes in that we must want it too. The individual human being makes "goodness" demonstrable.

Jesus called Peter to walk on the water. Peter could have said, "No." The miracle of Peter walking on water is seen in the courage of his "yes". As long as he had courage, it worked. When he began to doubt himself, he began to sink. The miracle for Peter was that for those few moments, he had divine courage. This is exactly what Nureyev did. He prayed for freedom. He wanted self-determination. He made a decision to defect for it. He left Russia, not because he wanted to dance, but because he wanted to dance with freedom. To dance is freedom. The miracle for Nureyev was that he knew what he wanted. He wanted it enough to risk everything for it. This is Spirituality. This is walking on water.

What has Spirituality to do with this? Everything. Spirituality is seeing all this fit together.

Seeing God in the confusions and decisions of life.
Seeing God in the never-ending doubts.
Seeing God in the daily acts of courage.

I want to explore a Spirituality that includes everybody and everything. A Spirituality that is connected with all aspects of living. A Spirituality that is the miracle of life.

Walking on Water

The magic of life.
The "mysterium tremendum".
The divine event that makes special our lives.
Spirituality is creative living.
Spirituality is experiencing our own personal power. Experiencing the confidence of knowing we have the power to bring every good feeling into our lives. A power that is not paranoid or selfish.
Not cruel,
"proudful,
unworthy", but appreciates the abilities and individual gifts we have all been given.
The energy of adolescence and youth that constantly challenges, seeking new, and often outrageous insights into living.
Marriage and friendships that produce the qualities of love, tolerance and loyalty.
Craftsmen working with wood or clay continue the Genesis drama of creation.
Musicians and song writers reflect the joys and sorrows of life.
The selfless patience of age and maturity that encourage the young with the contribution of wisdom.
In all these aspects of life is the Spirituality of being human.
Nowhere is creative Spirituality seen more clearly than in the specifically-human gift of humor. The genius, Albert Einstein, was once asked at a social gathering to explain his Theory of Relativity. He said, "Madam, I was once walking in the country on a hot day with a blind friend, and remarked that I would like a drink of milk. 'I understand drink,' said my friend, 'but what is milk?' 'A white liquid,' I replied. 'I know liquid, but what is white?' 'The same color as a swan's feathers.' 'I know feathers, but what is a swan?' 'A bird with a crooked neck.' 'I know neck, but what is crooked?' I lost my patience, I seized his arm and straightened it. Then I bent it at the elbow and said, 'That is crooked.' 'Ah,' said my blind companion, 'now I know what you mean by milk.' "[3] For those with eyes to see, Spirituality is everywhere. And it's okay to laugh.
Spirituality involves the journey into our real selves. Willingly wanting to face all that we will discover . . .
the good and the bad;
the courage and the fear;
the saint and the sinner . . .
Realizing and accepting that what is in us will also be in others. What is in us is life.

As the French writer, Necondale, says, "Human beings cannot, while they live, be rid of life." Once we begin to discover and accept these things, we have our finger on the power of the universe.

So long as we are in touch with life, we cannot remove ourselves from life. In this sense, I hope my book is helpful to those millions of people who are suffering from the disease of addiction . . . those people in all parts of the world who have addictive personalities and compulsive behavior habits that make them want to seek escape from their true selves.

In the everyday language of the drug addict, we see the "Great Lie" exposed. The "getting spaced" experience is nothing less than a continued isolation from reality. The "trip" is nothing less than a journey away from who they are. The "getting high" is another way of saying, "I am not good enough."

Being a recovering alcoholic, I know the real feelings behind this fantasy language. I know what it is to search for meaning in a drug . . . seek an answer in a drink . . . crave for happiness in a buzz. It is but an escape from reality.

In my trying to please and satisfy, the world lost me. In placing power "out there," I became a slave. In struggling to make my insides match society's outsides, I did not fit. For years, I lived the "great lie" of addiction.

Today I meet people who acknowledge that they got "high" and were "spaced" on food,
gambling,
and sick emotional attachment.

They used "something", and progressively became lost, angry, afraid and resentful.

Let the reader be the thermometer of his real needs.

A friend of mine made the comment, "Leo, you are implying that almost everyone has the disease of addiction."

I replied, "Yes, look at the pain, loneliness and mindless violence. The obsessions with sex, food, money and people— not to mention alcohol and drugs. If the disease of addiction in our society remains untreated, it will destroy our society."

I still believe this to be true.

The healing rests in the belief and confidence we have in ourselves. Do you believe that you can move mountains? Your belief will be dependent upon your seeing that such power is not located in the physical moving of mountains, but in knowing that you were created to create.

This miracle of "seeing" has nothing to do with the cover of this book and my getting wet in the ocean. It has to do with my knowing deep in myself that I am walking on water when I am truly centered in myself. Knowing that I was created to live, that I belong to this world, and the world belongs to me.

Wherever I am, that is where the center of the universe is.

Wherever I am, that is where meaning has its beginning.

To know that I have a purpose in this world; to know in every fiber of my being that I am important and unique; to know that without me the world would not be the same; to actually know that I make that much difference: *That* is walking on water.

To know that when the music is played, or the song is sung, you are involved and it lives through you. In a real way, you make what it is happen. In some mysterious and miraculous way, you are extending that creation and creating through it. It is all emanating from you. That your being here is making the difference. To actually know this is to walk on water.

To know as you walk through the forest or up a mountain that in some real and unique way it is part of you and belongs to you. To know that anything that destroys and mutilates part of nature in some way destroys and mutiliates part of you. To actually know this is to walk on water.

To know that the words we use are bridges of human contact, miracles of meaning by which ideas and feelings are expressed. To know that to stick rigidly and inflexibly to the word-meaning, is often to miss reality and lose the idea. If the "Sabbath was made for man", so was the "Word". To take that word or phrase and shake it around, jump on it, kick it in the dust, and dress it in "difference", is the creation of something new and different. This is what all great poets, writers and artists do. They take the ordinary and make it extraordinary. They take the everyday and make it special. They take the present and reveal the future.

George Steiner said of Shakespeare, "Shakespeare at times seems to hear inside a word or phrase the echo of the future."

To know this is to walk on water.

Somewhere in this adventure and confusion that we call life— is meaning. Somewhere in this pain, tension and death that we call existence—is meaning. Somewhere in this mixed togetherness of great men and fools, tyrants and saints—is meaning.

This is Spirituality.

The blind man, when healed, still had to plant the seed and hoe the ground, wash his face and clean between his toes. Lazarus, after returning from the dead, still needed to live with his arrogance and pride. He still needed to pray for others and ask forgiveness. Perhaps these everyday aspects of living reveal the "greater miracle".

Miracle is not found only in Grand Events. Great mystics and prophets need to eat, sleep, breathe, bathe and listen to others. Miracle is to be found in the quiet place, the ordinary, the gentle word and the welcoming smile.

We cannot walk on water unless we are prepared to risk, prepared to let go, "take courage" and plunge out. This is the story of Peter on the lake with Jesus.

The way forward is to risk freedom. I have been promised nothing less than the stars.

Years after his defection, Rudolf Nureyev said in an interview, "I am not one who is going to redo society, but I am going to show them where it is, which way to go. Reaching for something because reaching is something, rather than telling, for me is important."

This is Spirituality.

This is Walking on Water.

[1] *The Good News Bible* (with Deuterocanonicals/Apocrypha), St. Matthew 14:23-31.
[2] *Nureyev*, Clive Barnes.
[3] *The Wit of the Jews*, compiled by Lore and Maurice Cowan.

2 MIRACLE

Earlier in this book, I talked briefly about Lazarus. He was the man in St. John's Gospel whom Jesus brought back from the dead. It was a popular miracle at the time. Everybody knew about the raising of Lazarus. It still is a popular miracle amongst Christians.

It speaks of the power of God.

Resurrection.

New Life.

God loving His creation.

Lazarus had been dead for three days. St. John adds the realistic comment, "He stinketh." He was still bandaged in his burial clothes after he had been raised from the dead. He was dead, and yet he answered Jesus' call. Interestingly, Jesus tells Lazarus' sisters to untie him. Take care of him. He had not eaten anything for three days. The natural within the miracle. The Supernatural wrapped in common sense. This kind of incident is what most people expect miracles to be like.

Coming back from the dead.

Different.

Beyond belief.

. A miracle.

Something extraordinary.

Dividing seas.

Making blind people see.
Walking on water.
Another example is David and Goliath. This Old Testament story says something good about the little guy. I like this story. I am five feet, seven inches tall!

The mighty Philistine army is fighting against Israel and they send out their warrior giant, Goliath. Israel is asked to do the same. Unfortunately, Israel has no one comparable in size. This is little David's big chance. David may be short in size, but he is big on risk. David is chosen to represent Israel against Goliath.

> *Goliath started walking toward David again, and David ran quickly toward the Philistine battleline to fight him. He reached into his bag and took out a stone, which he slung at Goliath. It hit him on the forehead and broke his skull, and Goliath fell face downward on the ground. And so, without a sword, David defeated and killed Goliath with a sling and a stone! He ran to him, stood over him, took Goliath's sword out of its sheath, and cut off his head and killed him.*[1]

Goliath has complete body and head protection. He carries a huge shield and long sword. He looks fierce. He is tough. Only his face is left unprotected so that he can see.

By contrast, David goes into battle with a loose-fitting tunic, carrying only a sling. He takes five flat stones. This is Godly courage. Some people might call it insanity!

The mighty colossus wields his weapon. David feels the breeze from the giant's swishing sword. He concentrates. He selects his stone. Slings the sling. A direct hit. Goliath is struck in the temple. He falls. David chops off his head. Goliath is dead. A miracle.

Let me now describe a modern miracle. It concerns a fat lady. Elizabeth is suffering from obesity. She has suffered with an eating disorder for many years. She is 34. She decides to go into the hospital. She slowly begins to trust the staff at the hospital. A doctor understands her. Counselors share that they used to be like her. She sees other patients struggling with honesty. She trys to be honest. She develops a love and respect for the hospital program.

She begins to trust. It is not easy. She remembers. She cries. At times she asks, "Why?" Painful things are said. Hurts are uncovered and discovered.

At times Elizabeth feels scared.

She wonders if it is a waste of time and money.

Elizabeth wants to run away.

In spite of these doubts, she continues to trust. Continues to love and be loved. She experiences tough love—a day at a time. Her love and her trust grow. She begins to listen. She begins to hear.

Often she can take a compliment.

Occasionally she gives a compliment.

Now she stays for the compliment.

She hears the messages from the counselors:

"Elizabeth, I see the beauty in your face. In your eyes. Let me see the beauty inside."

"We love you. We see your pain. We hear you. Hear your loneliness. We love you."

"At times the disease will say to you, 'You are no good. You don't deserve all this attention.' However, the healthy side of you wants to be loved. Needs the attention. Wants to share the pain and get better. The healthy side of you is the real you."

"Elizabeth, you are a miracle. Long before the sickness began you were God's miracle. In the disease, you are still God's miracle. God creates miracles. God created you. You are God's miracle."

All these messages she hears. This in itself is a miracle. She hears compliments. She begins to trust. After years of silence and hiding, she begins to talk about her disease. About her pain. About her fatness.

She explains her loneliness as a child. Her father's drunken affection. That indelicate touch. Mother's cold glance. The constant criticism. The violence. The "put-down". The neglect. The isolation . . . Elizabeth puts out all her pain.

During her childhood, Elizabeth learned how to eat. Eating brought satisfaction. Comfort. Relief. More eating, more comfort. Enormous eating. Enormous satisfaction. She sneaked food. She hid food. Minimized amounts. Food became her protection from people. Protection from pain. Protection from criticism. Eventually, food took her on a "trip" away from her pain, away from reality.

Elizabeth spoke about her understanding of religion. It told her she was a sinner . . . needing repentance . . . needing salvation. She was told that she was no good without Jesus . . . without the Holy Spirit . . . without the Bible. The conditions of Heaven were purity and obedience. Her fears were perceived as guilt. Being human became a sin. However, nothing was said about food. Sex was a sin . . . thinking sex was terrible . . . nothing was said about food. Alcohol was a sin. Drugs were a sin. Nothing was said about food. It was okay to eat. Eating was good. Eating felt good and more was better.

Elizabeth was such a good eater. Elizabeth's eating made her grandmother proud. Grandmother told Elizabeth she was chubby and happy . . . fat people are happy. She wanted to stay happy, so she ate.

When Elizabeth went to visit friends, she learned how to please people. She ate all the meat. All the cake. They all smiled. She painfully remembered that she once said, "No more." Everybody looked disappointed. Had she insulted the host? Guilt. Feelings of rejection. She would never say "no more" again. Never disappoint grandmother. Never disappoint her friends again. She learned how to eat everything and vomit afterwards. Always in anger, guilt, loneliness or fear she would return to food. Even when her anger, guilt and loneliness were caused by food, she would return to food. Everything revolved around food.

In the hospital, Elizabeth began to talk out this story. She saw her disease come alive in her written words. She wrote down her feelings and owned them. She discovered forgotten feelings. Feelings she had swallowed with food. Buried with the food. Hidden in the food. Elizabeth faced reality, then she cried.

She came to see, understand, and accept the disease process. Her drug is food. Like a drinking alcoholic, she would hide it. Deny it. Lie about it. Lose her job because of it. Get divorced for it. Suffer using it. Food was her mind-altering drug. Food instantly works. Food brings satisfaction. Food is instant escape. That is Addiction.

Elizabeth's recovery and treatment begins when she sees this, feels this, accepts this.

Elizabeth feels her pain.

Feels her addiction.

Feels her disease.

Elizabeth was not a bad, crazy, ugly, sinful, irresponsible girl and woman. She was sick. She needed help. She felt she was utterly alone. In the hospital, she met fellow sufferers. People who were being treated for the same disease. The symptoms were the same. The pain the same. Growing numbers of people were demanding recognition for their disease.

In a treatment center, we helped Elizabeth treat her disease. However, Elizabeth must do the work, make recovery happen, bring about the miracle. Without Elizabeth's energy and cooperation, we could do nothing except give a diet. That would be like treating a bullet wound with a band-aid. A severe burn with Vaseline. Elizabeth needed more. When a patient needs surgery, you do not give a pill. Elizabeth needed surgery.

In order to create a realistic food program, we needed from Elizabeth honesty,
> willingness,
>> cooperation.

We needed to hear her stuffed feelings:
> fear,
>> resentment,
>>> loneliness
>>>> and anger.

We needed Elizabeth to see that in these feelings was the disease. The food was the symptom. All the pain, all the feelings of being "less than", all the people-pleasing had to be seen and owned. All the denial, the manipulation, the self-pity had to be seen and owned. This is treatment.

The gentle art of loving yourself was introduced. This is the process and the program. The treatment and recovery are for life. Loving yourself begins when you see your power; your freedom; your right to choose.

Loving yourself begins when you feel your power,
> feel your freedom,
>> feel your right to choose.

This is Spirituality. This is miracle.

Elizabeth has no choice about having the disease. She did not choose it. She did not do anything to deserve it. She certainly did not ask for it. However, she has it. That is reality. It is part of her. She can accept it, work on it, live with it a day at a time—or deny it and die. That is reality. For Elizabeth to know this is to bring power, freedom, and miracle into her life. To live is to have choice. The wrong choice gives power to the disease. The right choice keeps the power with Elizabeth.

She is free to eat destructively and die.
> She is free to eat positively and live.

The power and recovery rest in the feelings behind Elizabeth's eating. At whom is she eating? Is she eating on anger or guilt? Where is Elizabeth in her eating? If she is positive about her life, positive about her health, positive about her disease, she will choose the foods that love her. Choose balanced food habits. Choose to eat to live rather than live to eat. To experience good feelings does not require food. Abstinence, meaning a balanced and selected food program, must be practiced for continued recovery. Elizabeth must choose a style of eating that is good for her; meal plans that bring health.

For Elizabeth, the treatment was in giving her the knowledge to discover herself. Share herself. Be the creative human being she was meant to be. Today, she has discovered that creative Spirituality that comes with being real. Today, she is comfortable with herself. Loved and loving in her new relationships. Confident in who she is. Creating a new life. Making her own world. Living in the solution — not the problem. Accepting the support and program of Overeaters Anonymous. Oh, yes, and she is getting slimmer. Elizabeth is walking on water.

Another miracle. People can miss the miracle of Elizabeth because they have a narrow view of God's activity. They make miracle too exclusive.

Miracle is Lazarus. A man coming back from the dead.

Miracle is Bartimaeus. A blind man seeing.

Miracle is David. Killing the giant Goliath with a stone.

But Elizabeth. Elizabeth is a wonderful story about courage and perseverance. No more and no less!

I say more. I say much more. Elizabeth's story is a miracle. Indeed Elizabeth is a miracle.

We make God too small.

We make miracle too small.

We make human beings too small.

People are so busy looking for God, they miss Him. His world. In you and me.

Two men were talking in a bar. The atheist said, "There is no such thing as God."

The other man said, "Why do you say that?"

The Atheist continued, "I asked His help once when I was stuck in the desert. Dying in the glaring sun. I cried out for God's help!"

The other man said, "Something must have happened. You are here now."

"Not really," said the atheist. "Some crazy Indian came and saved me!"

The traces of the Creator are in the created. We reflect the Divine. In us is the Divine seen. In our action is the Divine event. We are the miracle. This is what the atheist missed.

So many people see miracles as God doing something to somebody. God working a miracle on somebody. Something "out there" brought "down here". Miracle is seen only as a Divine Intervention. The parting of the Red Sea or Saul's experience on the Damascus road. These events happen rarely. Today, few people really expect miracles.

I expect miracles and see miracles. The most common miracle is our capacity to cooperate. We can make things happen. We can create. We make miracles.

Instead of waiting for it . . . make it happen.

Instead of waiting for God . . . experience Him.

Instead of waiting for a miracle . . . realize you are it.

People confuse miracle with magic. Magic is a trick, the pretended art of spells, charms and rituals, done to amaze, entertain or control a group of people. Magic is illusion and clever deceit. An unreal experience that confuses. Magic keeps the power with the magician or witch doctor or wizard. We, the people, are spectators, not participants. We make no contribution. We add nothing. We are helpless victims of the magician's power and spells.

Many religious people, in ignorance, pray for magic. Want magic, ask for magic. It reminds me of Jesus' desert temptations at the beginning of His ministry.

Jesus returned from the Jordan full of the Holy Spirit, and was led by the Spirit into the desert, where he was tempted by the Devil for forty days. In all that time, he ate nothing, so that he was hungry when it was over.

The Devil said to him, "If you are God's Son, order this stone to turn into bread."

But Jesus answered, "The scripture says man cannot live on bread alone."

Then the Devil took him up and showed him in a second all the kingdoms of the world. "I will give you all this power and all this wealth," the Devil told him. "It has all been handed over to me, and I can give it to anyone I choose. All this will be yours, then, if you worship me."

Jesus answered, "The scripture says Worship the Lord your God and serve only him!"

Then the Devil took him to Jerusalem and set him on the highest point of the Temple, and said to him, "If you are God's Son, throw yourself down from here. For the scripture says, 'God will order his angels to take good care of you.' It also says, 'They will hold you up with their hands so that not even your feet will be hurt on the stones.' "

But Jesus answered, "Do not put the Lord your God to the test."

When the Devil finished tempting Jesus in every way, he left him for a while.[2]

What kind of Messiah was He going to be? Would He feed the poor by changing stones into bread? No!

Would He do a deal with the Devil to gain political power over all the Kingdoms? No!

Would He offer circus spectacles from Temple roofs? No!

Jesus would offer no such mighty signs. No theatricals. No magic. So many religious people forget this message and seek the supernatural fix. They want God to work the trick in their lives.

Take away the problems.

Remove the sickness or disease.

Stop the divorce.

Get Alice through college.

Keep George off the booze.

"God, will you work the magic?"

God is the universal drug of choice. Get high on religion. The Jesus trip. Say the prayer and the pain is gone. For a while it seems to work. But it does not last. It is not real.

Miracle requires cooperation.

It demands something from us.

It requires our investment.

Ask and you shall receive.

Seek and you shall find.

Knock and the door will be opened.

You must do something.

Back to Lazarus. He answered Jesus' call in death as he had in life. He obeyed in death as he had obeyed in life. Jesus' desire to use him as a sign of life after death, a sign of miracle within life, happens because Lazarus cooperated beyond the grave. I do not doubt the immensity of God's power working through Jesus . . . but Lazarus also had power. If Jesus worked hard, so did Lazarus. Remember, it was Lazarus who struggled in his burial bandages to walk. Then Jesus said to Lazarus' sisters, "Unbind him and let him go."

In the bandages and the concern to untie him is the natural miracle. Had this been magic instead of "miracle" it would have produced a dazzling Lazarus that would have danced out of the grave.

The miracle of David in the face of the giant, Goliath, is his courage, determination and skill as a marksman. David believes that God is with him. Believes that God will spare Israel. David is prepared to fight for his beliefs. David makes the miracle happen. He cooperates. He gets involved.

Notice how David chooses the weapon with which he is comfortable, the sling. King Saul had wanted David to wear his armour and carry his kingly sword. David declined. He selected five flat stones. Stood his ground in the face of Goliath's taunts. David cooperated with God's will and produced the miracle. Magic would not have required a sling and flat stones. Magic would not have required human hunting skills. With magic, David would have puffed Goliath out of existence while peeling a grape!

My understanding of miracle involves the human being. It requires cooperation and involvement. Miracle comes when we are prepared to "grasp".

It is the exercise of human power,
                    human freedom,
                              human choice.
This is what Elizabeth realized in treatment.

The miracle of life is to be lived. People who get the most out of life are those people who put the most into it.

The poet, C. Day-Lewis said, "Earth is your talent. Use it." Do not wait for things to happen, make them happen. Those people who have made positive contributions to the world, inspired change, stimulated human understanding, and brought about the creation of justice, have all believed in themselves. Believed in their power. Made things happen. Martin Luther King had a dream and lived his dream; his dream involved human dignity for all men. Martin Luther King enabled others to dream. Where was the miracle? I say in him.

The same for Mahatma Ghandi. He worked for freedom. He worked for Indian dignity. He worked for lasting peace and justice. All without violence. Where was the miracle? In him. Being the miracle, he made the miracle happen.

So with Mother Teresa; she epitomizes the nobility of life. Proclaims the beauty of life in death. No child will die in her arms without love. Where is the miracle? In her. Being the miracle, she makes the miracle happen.

Countless men and women from all races, religions and creeds reveal the miracle of being human. What is the difference between them and you? Perhaps for a moment or longer you forgot to believe in yourself. You forgot to believe in your miracle. Think about it. Who is stopping your being what you want to be but you? You want to be a painter, then go buy the books, brushes, paints— and go to school. You want to play the piano, learn a foreign language, ride a bike, write a book . . .? Then go make your dream come true. Make the miracle!

Remember the blind man in the Gospel? He received the miracle of sight from Jesus, but he first had to shout for it. There were many blind men in Jerusalem, but his difference was in his SHOUT. He shouted his need so loudly that Jesus heard. His shout produced the miracle. People in the crowd told him to shut up. Be quiet. The blind man refused to listen to others. His "people-pleasing" days were over. Other blind and crippled people obeyed the crowd. The blind man cried louder. They did not get it. He got it. I ask you, would he have received his sight, had he not shouted?

There were many lepers in Judea, and yet the lepers who were cleansed were those who walked for it. For miles they walked on their crippled little feet. In the walking was the miracle. They walked, they asked, they received.

What are you looking for in your life? What are your needs? The answers will be found within you. God created and is creating. When we are at our most positive, most receptive, most real, we are cooperating with His will for us. We unite with Him. We become ONE. These moments of miracle are constantly being offered to us, but we do not always realize it. We are hooked into destructive power. We are centered in self pity. We neglect our creative energy.

Have you ever stopped to consider how small we think? We get dulled by the machinery of life, and we miss the adventure, the fun, the freedom. While I am writing, I see the stars in the sky and I get in touch with belonging to something much bigger than my little world. The Universe is incredible. The world is a mystery. And I am an important part of it.

Take the example of my Christian religion. I recently realized that the Mass is not just the Last Supper. It is not the ritual or ceremony. It is not what the priest does with bread and wine. As Christians, we are not there simply to remember yesterday or worship a dead hero. The Mass is alive. It is the people. We, the

people, do the Mass and make the Sacrament. We meet as the
Body of Christ, to share the Body of Christ, to live as the Body of
Christ. Jesus did not live, die, and rise again for bread and wine.
Jesus brought God's power to the people. The Mass is the miracle
of the people. Whatever truth is in the liturgy, it must be lived out
in the world. The words of the Bible must be given flesh and
blood in our lives. Whatever absolution I receive must be lived out
in the forgiveness I offer to others and myself. I am the Mass.

For years I thought the Mass was a magic service. I was too busy
making "miracle" that I lost the miracle. I could not see God for
the Church.

I was made to see my wretched smallness when a Muslim child
offered me bread in Tunisia. In the child's eyes, I saw love. The
miracle of God's oneness was lost in my parochial smallness. I
knew the Christian rules. I forgot God.

In the gift of life is the miracle given. God created the miracle
in you and me, and He invites us to create. The wisdom comes in
knowing we have the power. The power to heal our lives. The
power to begin again.

The following story explains where the power comes from:

A man dies and goes to Heaven. He sees the door marked
"God's Kingdom" and so he knocks.

God speaks from within and asks, "Who is it?"

The man replies, "It is I."

God says, "You cannot come in."

"I must be doing something wrong," thinks the man.

Again he goes to the door marked "God's Kingdom" and
knocks.

"Who is it?" asks God.

"It is I," says the man.

God says, "You cannot come in."

Finally, the man stops and thinks for a long time. He smiles. He
goes to the door and knocks again.

God says, "Who is it?"

"It is You."

"Come in," says God.

> To know this is to walk on water.

---

[1] *Good News Bible,* Today's English Version, I Samuel 17:48-51.
[2] *Good News Bible,* Today's English Version, St. Luke 4:1-3.

3 | SPIRITUALITY

Two frightened little fish were huddled together in the ocean, afraid to move. Out of the deep lagoon came a large, beautiful fish with a glittering body. He was brimming over with confidence and began to pass the two little fish with great force. He noticed their shivering forms, and turned to them and said, "Why stay huddled together? Why don't you swim out into the clear, glistening water?" The two little fish looked at each other, and then one of them said, "Where is the water?"

This story highlights the problem facing many people. They are in life, and yet they are not living. You only begin to live when you recognize life.

They know deep inside that they are missing something.

They know deep inside they were not created to hide.

They know deep inside that the magic of life is escaping them; yet, how to get it? Where is the water of life? The two little fish were huddled together, shaking with fear, and not doing anything.

Fear tends to do this to people.

Fear makes people frozen.

Scared stiff.

Petrified.

Fear keeps people prisoners of themselves. The fear of rejection. The fear of not being understood. The fear of being considered too small, not good enough, not intelligent, or too plain. The wrong color,
　　　　　　　religion,
　　　　　　　　　race.
All these fears group together to keep a person afraid and alone.

I suppose it is the difference between existing and living. Existing is what the two little fish were doing. Things happened around them, but they were unwilling to make things happen for themselves. They ask questions, rather than seek answers. The little fish never initiated anything. They never did anything. They were prisoners of their frightened existence.

Many people are like this. For any number of reasons, they will not try new things, new experiences, and different happenings. They will not venture into new territories. The statement, "I have never done that," becomes the reason for never trying it. This is the barrier that stops a person from experiencing new people, new ideas, new places, something different. Good experiences like going to the theatre, inviting friends for dinner, eating Chinese food, or visiting a foreign country never happen because "I have never done that." The fear of the unknown.

This fear stops the experience of life, and it is self-imposed. It does not exist apart from ourselves. We create it and sustain it. We make our own fears and bring them into our lives. It is the "boogeyman" syndrome; the fears are products of our sick and frightened imaginations.

Life is not lived, it is endured. Fear of not being good enough stops you from being anything.
　　　　　　Fear stops you from being somebody.
　　　　　　Fear stops you from being yourself.
We miss the joy of living by not taking risks.
　　　　We miss the freedom-experience,
　　　　　　the people-experience,
　　　　　　the love-experience,
　　the growth-experience, by waiting for life instead of seizing it.

How do we create this emptiness in our lives? By not saying "hello" on our morning walk or jog. By not telling the family that we are afraid or lonely. By thinking that people are talking about us. Or being afraid to speak, in case the words come out wrong. John Donne said, "No man is an island." Yet many people feel they are isolated pieces of humanity. And it is fear that creates this isolation.

Spirituality is the way out of this prison. It is the key that opens the door to yourself, and the exciting journey of life. Your life. When I give lectures about Spirituality, people always ask, "How do I get it? How can I bring Spirituality into my life? Is there a teach-yourself book?" These questions miss the essential point about Spirituality; SPIRITUALITY HAS ALREADY BEEN GIVEN! You and I have it. We are spiritual creatures, and the emphasis should not be on "getting it" or "obtaining it" but on "DISCOVERING IT". The answer is in opening the window and experiencing life. Life is to be experienced.

Spirituality is reality. I am aware of my Spirituality when I am being real. Spirituality is my body, mind, emotions and style. That essence of my being that makes sense to me and is personal to me. The more honest I can get, the more I understand and am understood. Of course this honesty can be a frightening experience. When honesty is being experienced, then vulnerability is felt. Honesty is not just me telling people "things", it is me giving them me. Also, they, the listeners, by their eyes, smiles, intermittent "I know," give me something of their lives. Scary stuff!

The more I share the real me, the more I can know the real you. In an honest conversation, I share and you bleed. Or you share and I bleed. The courageous part is the initial risk. Trusting. Letting go. God sees our situation more clearly than we do, and to flow with His will for us we must be prepared to "let go" of old attitudes, ideas, people and things. A story told at Alcoholics Anonymous meetings clearly reveals this:

Once upon a time, a man fell over a cliff. As he was falling, he reached out and grabbed at a branch. As he hung there, he shouted, "God, if you really do exist, please get me out of this mess."

A voice said, "This is God speaking. Please follow my directions carefully. One, let go of the tree."

At this the man shouted back, "Is there anyone else up there?" What God saw that the man could not see was a wide ledge a few feet below him. Let go and live.

Most times we are not in contact with our God-given Spirituality. We miss it, reject it, or ignore it. The time and occasions that we make contact, those wonderful occasions when we feel and touch the very essence of our life-flow, we glow with enthusiasm. At

Let Go — Let God

such moments it is great to be alive. It is not only great to be alive, it is great to be who we are and alive.

Such moments are abundant in our lives, but we often miss them. We concentrate on clutter, the superficial, the unreal, and we miss the beauty that has been given. The splendor of life.

Are you in touch with your life? Are you there in your life? If you answer, "Yes," then you are already aware of the thrill of living. The wonder of living. That constant joy in Spirituality. It is always to be found in the real.

When two people are in love, it is loudly present. It shouts from their eyes, faces and sprightly walk. Love is overflowing, demanding attention. It radiates from the most discreet, respectable and proper people. It cannot be hidden or disguised. When two people are in love, life is filled with meaning and everything is exciting.

The shared telephone call between young lovers and the nervous pronunciation of the name send shivers down the listening lover's spine. The meal and walk in the park become a sacramental communion that radiates a real presence. Even the making up after a silly argument becomes a joyous experience of generous forgiveness. Love makes everything exciting, meaningful and extraordinary.

A young man who has been an isolated prisoner of his homosexual feelings throughout his adolescence meets another man who says he feels the same. Yes, the other man actually says he feels the same way. The young man is not alone. He is not the only one with such feelings. The other man says he wants to be a friend. Over a period of time, they become lovers. That experience is spiritual. The once-argued dirty touch is transformed into a caress of love. The pulsating bodily feelings that yesterday's religious men denounced as sinful are expressed in the healing sensations of a mature sexuality. The love that dared not speak its name has a confident message for a frightened people.

All over the world, different and separate minorities find hope in the risks a brave few are prepared to take. They find the courage to crawl out of their guilt-ridden prisons to breathe the free and fresh air of being who they are. Yes, the other man feels the same! That moment of Spirituality is discovered in a new and different love.

The old widower at the Senior Citizen's Club who finds in the widow, Mabel, a meaning and purpose to the latter days of his life is another whisper of this given love. Their comforting talk of how things used to be, the shared pride in their children, their doubled strength as they walk towards death, are aspects of this Spirituality that is given. The sparkling crinkled eyes of these two people tells the story that began yesterdays ago, and will end in forever.

The Jewish family that adopts the Arab boy. The young Oxford graduate who offers three years' work in an underdeveloped country are other whisperings of this loving life force. It is all around, but rarely noticed. Yet, look without and within, and it must be seen.

It was the toys in *The Velveteen Rabbit* who found the secret of love:

> *"What is REAL?" asked the rabbit one day, when they were lying side-by-side near the nursery fender, before Nana came to tidy the room. "Does it mean having things that buzz inside you and a stick-out handle?"*
>
> *"Real isn't how you are made," said the skin horse. "It's a thing that happens to you. When a child loves you for a long, long time, not just to play with, but really loves you, then you become REAL."*
>
> *"Does it hurt?" asked the rabbit.*
>
> *"Sometimes," said the skin horse, for he was always truthful. "When you are real, you don't mind being hurt."*
>
> *"Does it happen all at once, like being wound up?" he asked, "or bit by bit?"*
>
> *"It doesn't happen all at once," said the skin horse. "You BECOME. It takes a long time. That's why it doesn't happen to people who break easily or have sharp edges, or who have to be carefully kept. Generally by the time you are REAL, most of your hair has been loved off, and your eyes drop out, and you get loose in the joints and very shabby. But these things don't matter at all, because once you are REAL, you can't be ugly, except to people who don't understand."*[3]

In every life, Spirituality is to be discovered. We have all had such moments. My definition for Spiritualty is "That which enables and develops positive and creative forces in a human being."

God is against sin because it does not work! By sin, I mean destructive and negative forces that corrupt what is noble in man. History is full of tyrants and bullies who achieved political power, and yet what they plotted and killed for is no longer with us. Hate may be remembered, but it does not inspire. Spirituality is the essential remedy for all destructive and negative attitudes, because it produces positive and creative lifestyles. Great lovers are great leaders. To be a leader, you must be a lover.

If the little fish at the beginning of this chapter would only love themselves, they would be swimming in the living waters of life.

This Spirituality, this creative love, affects and transforms the whole personality. Spirituality makes the loving couple zealous for life.

It makes guilt-ridden gays positive and accepting.

It makes aged and crippled bodies gentle and hopeful.

These people are no longer preoccupied with what others think or say about them. They have accepted themselves. Instead of the prison of fear, they are in the flow of positive thinking.

The prison comes from having no love of ourselves. Very early in our lives, many of us learned from family, school and church what we should not be. What we should not reveal. We are told what we should not feel. What we should not do.

And when we feel or do things we were told not to feel or do, then we feel guilty and ashamed.

To live in conformity, we learn how to block out reality. Kill off the feelings. Act out a role. In blocking out the feelings, we block out our true selves. Soon nothing is left. When asked how we feel, we look vacant. We are vacant. We are not at home.

The children who were taught how to block out feelings become the adults with blank expressions and negative attitudes about life; the emotional game-players in society.

A narrow and biased education produces religious and sexual prejudices that later cause conflict and division in society.

Hypocritical attitudes are developed in a community that encourages and rewards only achievement and success. The ruling minority decides what it wants and what is acceptable.

The casualties from this social system are immense.

In the chance remark of a grandparent or teacher, the Mexican boy is taught how to see himself as "different", "less than", "secondary".

The Jew is expected to keep to himself.

The Black looks different, but is encouraged not to talk about it.

Daughters are encouraged to obey religiously strict fathers, and wives "play pretty" for their husbands.

Thousands are taught how to play games and please people rather than how to be real. So many people live a lie and exist to please. The creative and positive Spirituality that is given to the human being by God at birth is smothered and atrophied by guilt and fear. Life is now exchanged for existence. In such ways, diseased prisons are built and the tragedy is that most people are unaware that they not only live in them, but helped to create them.

Some of these prisons were erected under the influence of over-enthusiastic and sick religious fanatics. Priests and TV evangelists pressing guilt buttons to the tune of "Jesus Wants Me For a Sunbeam". Unexplained and uninterpreted Bible passages are used to condemn and control a variety of people; an exchange of personal power for cult dictatorship.

All religions are institutions built by men that often speak for God. Most religions have a power structure that involves creeds, holy writings, dogmas, priests and ministers, food laws, rules and regulations, an objective morality, and social customs that have all evolved from various ethnic traditions. Some religions, to their credit, have willingly accepted the customs of other cultures and developed together.

All religions are essentially earth-bound with Divine inter-ventions. Herein lies the dilemma; what is true? Is it all true because the Bible and tradition say so, or do we need an intelligent and sensitive interpretation? It can be clearly dem-onstrated that many of yesterday's dogmas have today been cast aside after the development of science and modern medicine. A study of religion often tells us more about the people who believe than the spiritual qualities that are believed in.

All religions have rules and teachings that encourage heavenly thoughts and aspirations, but also produce earthly prejudices and resentments. The Protestant and Catholic antagonism is a variation on the Arab and Jewish conflict, which can be compared with the Moslem and Hindu disagreements. Whatever ingredients are added to the religious cake for tasting, for the majority of people it seems to be a gastronomical mess. Spiritual people are wise to be on a severe religious diet!

An understanding of religion that I share is expressed by a Hindu teacher, the late Baba Muktanada, who had an Ashram in Oakland, California. He said:

> *Every religion is okay in its own right. There may be religions—not hundreds, but thousands of religions. Yet, how many Gods are there to bestow their grace upon all these religious people? God is one—He can't become two. Does God belong to the Hindus? Is He a Christian? Is He Jewish? Is*

*He a Sufi? Does He belong to Buddhism? Is He Black? Is He
White? Is He Red? To whom does He belong? This is the
important question, and it is worth contemplating.*
    *Now it is very likely that because He is God, He belongs to
everybody. For Hindus, He is Ram, and for Christians He is
called God. For Sufis He is Allah, and for Zoroastrians He is
Zarathustra. Everyone calls Him by a different name.*
    *After pursuing all these religions, we should learn how to
cultivate the awareness of Universal Brotherhood. Don't
pursue these religions so that we can murder one another
with distinctions. All countries belong to Him, all languages
belong to Him, all mantras belong to Him, and all religions
belong to Him. He belongs to everybody. All the people who
follow different religions should attain this understanding.* [2]

This understanding is Spirituality.

Spirituality is given. It is what it is to be a human being. It is that
given spark of creativity . . . yesterday's soul. Words change, but
the gift remains: It is that which is real about the human being.
You can live without religion, but you only exist without the
awareness of Spirituality.

How do you get in touch with your Spirituality? It is the
responsibility of every individual to seek, discover, and nurture
his/her own. You are responsible for you.

You are responsible for the joys and chaos you choose to make.

You are responsible for your life.

And that takes us close to the problem: many people will not
accept responsibility for themselves. We complain, we get angry,
we harbor resentments, and yet we do not see that we are bringing
the pain into our own lives. We perceive the world from our own
hernia!

My existence stems from where I am. Whether I choose to write
a book, go to work, or even consider it a good day, is dependent
upon my attitude. To miss this is to miss me. Miss my life.

The "good morning" in the park or the evening embrace are
dependent upon our attitude as individuals. In this sense, how
you stroke the dog can affect the business contract! How you
speak to your Mexican gardener affects your developing
Spirituality. Because I believe it is God's world and we are His, I
know that it is my world and your world. We are responsible for
everything in our world.

Spirituality Is Being Free

Baba Muktanada said, *"I am trying to help people feel God inside of them; wake up."*

The kind word can only be said if we choose to say it. That needed word of encouragement or forgiveness requires you. Others may say it, but that would not be you. It would not be you saying it. Remember, nobody can say it like you. You are terrific.

In your individuality is your uniqueness.

In your individuality is your power.

In your individuality is your divinity.

Everything stems from how you choose to practice your Spirituality. The word of encouragement or the silence of understanding.

All are part of life.

All are our responsibility.

Even the negative and critical statements are ours.

We choose to hurt.

We choose to be cruel.

We choose to destroy.

The awareness of our imperfections can be the way back to our given Spirituality. Jesus explained this attitude to life in the story about the priest and the sinner.

> *He also told this parable to some who trusted in themselves that they were righteous and despised others: "Two men went up into the temple to pray, one a Pharisee and the other a tax collector. The Pharisee stood and prayed thus with himself: 'God, I thank thee that I am not like other men, extortioners, unjust, adulterers, or even like this tax collector. I fast twice a week, I give tithes of all that I get.' But the tax collector, standing far off, would not even lift up his eyes to heaven, but beat his breast, saying, 'God, be merciful to me, a sinner!' I tell you, this man went down to his house justified rather than the other; for everyone who exalts himself will be humbled, but he who humbles himself will be exalted.'* [3]

Let me explain. I am an alcoholic. I do not know why I am alcoholic. Nobody in my immediate family is alcoholic. It is not something I ever seriously intended to be. Whether the disease is biological, psychological or environmental seems interesting only for after-dinner conversation. Such talk is redundant to my survival. The important fact is that I have the disease of alcoholism, and I had better accept it and live with it.

In simple terms, I cannot drink alcohol and get away with it. I have problems when I drink alcohol.

In real terms, alcohol was the way I avoided living with me. History teaches me this. My history of my drinking teaches me this.

I can choose to ignore it. I can choose to manipulate these facts. I can choose to make excuses. However, I will be the loser. To not take responsibility for my life is to go back to the disease. It is to give the disease power over me.

I now know and accept what I am. I am an alcoholic. Yesterday's games only hurt me and those who loved me. When I claimed to have fooled psychiatrists and bishops, I now see that I only fooled myself.

Now I see. I am the only thing that I have got. When I have me, I have everything. Without me, I have nothing. I really believe today that it would be insane to neglect, hurt or destroy the me, I mean all of me, with whom I have to work with. This is me.

It is good for family and friends to accept that I am alcoholic, but it is essential for me to know and accept it. Not only live with it, but accept the reality of the disease. Bring my alcoholism and my recovery into the living of my life. Make the disease work for me. Use the disease in my life to live.

The young couple in love used their relationship to experience a spiritual communion.

The widower and Mabel used their loving companionship to face death.

The young man's acceptance of his homosexuality brought freedom and growth to his life.

The acceptance of my disease brings spiritual growth into my life.

I really believe that Spirituality is given. It permeates the fabric of being human. The more I can discover about myself, the more love I can give myself. Love my alcoholism. Love and be responsible for that part of me that is diseased. Not to hurt me is to know me. That is Spirituality.

I tried to drink alcohol like other people and I ended up drinking alcohol like a drunk. I was never ordinary or balanced in my drinking. When I did manage to control my drinking at a dinner party, I always wanted more. God, the pain of trying to control! My insides screamed when I politely said, "Enough for me."

Now I know that the problem was not the alcohol, but the person drinking the alcohol. The drinking was the symptom of the sickness, but the real disease lived . . .

> in my loneliness,
>> guilt,
>>> feeling of isolation,
>> anger
>>> and personalized pain.

All these painful feelings were me. I hid the sickness behind a face of confidence and crazy merriment. Drinking only enabled me to escape to Fantasy Island and live the fantasy; and part of this escape was painful.

I always wanted to be like other people. I wanted my insides to feel like other people's outsides. I wanted to experience what you looked like. I wanted desperately to be loved and accepted by you. I would do anything, be anything, say anything to please you. I was living my life for you. I felt that without you, there was no me.

I was not tall enough. My brain was not good enough. My family was not rich enough.

I never wanted you to discover these feelings, so I hid them. Buried them deep within me. By being permanently on stage, I could keep the world out of my tragic life. I would only let you see what I wanted you to see.

Long before alcohol, I hid behind pretensions and lies. I could play games and weave webs that kept everybody who was concerned going in circles. Alcohol only added to the confusion and made me feel good. I drank myself into courage, elegance and brilliance. I was the next best thing to God. At times I was God!

The disease progressed and I was taken farther into the world of fantasy. Alcohol was taking me away from the uncomfortable world I had lived in for such a long time. When I experienced pain or a problem, I reached for my friend in the bottle. In a few gulps, I could exchange reality for fantasy. For the price of a bottle of gin, I could create my own world and keep the other world out. Alcohol was my fix. Alcohol was my drug of choice.

Some people use food. Others drugs and pills. Some get high on power and sexual conquests. Thousands play one drug against another, mix up the compulsions. The drug may vary, but the reason is the same: ESCAPE. The disease is the same for all these compulsions; it is preferring fantasy to a life in reality. The loneliness, isolation, fear of people and oneself is more telling about alcoholism than wet beds, car crashes and midnight brawls.

You can remove the alcohol from my alcoholic system, brain and lifestyle, but you cannot remove the alcohol "IC". It is the "IC" that wants me to drink again, escape again, people-please again, hand my power over again, run from pain again. The "IC" is that sick part of me that I need to take care of, be responsible for, seek to manage in my life. The only hook the "IC" needs to run rampant in my life is the desire to be unreal, the wish for fantasy, the urge to escape, the little white lie that supposedly nobody cares about. Once you want out of your life, the "IC" wants in.

Notice I have not mentioned being drunk. You do not need to drink to experience the insanity of a drunk. The alcoholic can still be suffering from the disease of alcoholism without having a physical drink. The temper tantrums, deceits, ego trips, aspects of denial, seeking to control and take charge of the lives of others, unresolved anger and resentments—all these are symptoms of the dry-drunk. Spirituality is not an interesting option for the addict: it is essential. It is the essence of his program for sobriety and peace of mind. A realized spirituality is daily recovery.

In the clear vision of surrender can be seen the latent stirrings of recovery and success. The creative bridge between human beings is the disclosure of our actions and attitudes we most dislike. In the open discussion of our darker side is the seed of creativity sown.

For many people, spiritual growth has come with the acceptance of a disease. The acceptance of something they cannot control in their lives. The acceptance of something that will destroy them if left untreated. The acceptance of addiction. This is the moment of a powerful and living spirituality. A. Alvariz says in his book, *The Shaping Spirit*, "There is a moment at which things come truly alive; the moment at which they are caught in all their subtlety by the imagination. They then take to themselves meaning."

Sharing is such a moment. My need to share, my need to tell you how I feel, my need to bleed with you keeps alive the reality of who I am and what I have. To let go of my resentments and destructive attitudes is the beginning of freedom. To let go and let God is to discover this given Spirituality.

The following poem was given to me by an anonymous recovering addict:

After a while you learn
the subtle difference

between holding a hand
and chaining a soul.
And you learn
that love doesn't mean leaning
and company doesn't mean security.
And you begin to learn
that kisses aren't contracts,
and presents aren't promises.
And you begin to accept your defeats
with your head up and your eyes ahead
    with the grace of a woman,
    not the grief of a child.
And you learn to build all your roads on today
    because tomorrow's ground is
    too uncertain for plans.
And futures have a way of falling down
    in mid-flight.
After a while, you learn
that even sunshine burns if you ask too much,
    so you plant your own garden
    and decorate your own soul,
Instead of waiting for someone to bring you flowers.
    And you learn
    that you really can endure,
    that you really are strong.
And you really do have worth.
    And you learn
        and you learn.
    With every good-bye
        you learn . . .

Norah—an anonymous woman in a Massachusetts prison

[1]Margery Williams, *The Velveteen Rabbit.*
[2]Jess Laird Book, p. 91.
[3]St. Luke 18:9-14.

4 | MY MOMENT

There are times — I want to call them "moments" — when you are given the opportunity to see and understand who you really are. I know that the one special moment I wish to describe occurred after my last drunken car crash. I left the bar at three in the afternoon and almost made it home. I was seconds from my home in England when I crashed my car and was almost killed. That catastrophe became an opportunity to experience something I needed to know. From the debris of a car crash, I had a moment of sanity.

A moment when I could see something.

A moment when I could know something.

A moment when I could grow.

I came in touch with the real world.

I had a glimpse of the real Leo. I am not saying this was the first time I was aware of being drunk; that was a common experience! The miracle of this moment was that it was the first time I was aware of having a serious problem.

Aware I was sick.

Aware I was alcoholic.

A moment of suffering became an opportunity for growth and joy. What I share in this book has its roots in that happening some years ago.

My Moment

In that special moment after the car crash, I saw my alcoholic fantasy.

My insane drama.

My erratic impulses.

My absolute loneliness and utter isolation.

I emerged from the crash realizing something I had denied for years: I was an alcoholic.

Let me say that again and bring it into today.

I AM an alcoholic.

Amid the shouts and screams from women with perambulators, motorists trying to redirect cars around smouldering metal, mumblings from a growing audience staring at a drunken priest with his head between his knees at the side of the road, a part of me was saying:

"You know you really are an alcoholic."

"Problems happen when you drink."

"Your drinking will ruin your life and destroy you."

"What are you going to do?"

But the most constant theme in my mind's group committee meeting was: "You are an alcoholic."

At some point, a flash of sanity answered these voices by saying: "Yes, I know I am an alcoholic."

I am not saying that I completely surrendered. That I fully accepted or understood the implications of my alcoholism. I was no St. Paul on the Damascus Road with a voice from Jesus halting me in my tracks. Oh, no! I heard no voices from The Beyond.

These voices came from within:

"You are an alcoholic."

While all this was happening, I experienced the uncanny, strange feeling of standing outside of myself, seeing the confusion, the horror with startling clarity, and looking at me— drunk— with my head between my legs. From above the smoke and noise, I stared at me. I had never seen me quite like this before. Oh, yes, I had often caught myself drunk before, caught myself in the act of drunken rage or vicious sarcasm, I had even stopped myself from banging doors or smashing china—but I had never seen me like I was seeing me now.

I knew that the drunk at the side of the road was not the real me.

I knew that the priest who loved his work, loved God's world and loved people, was within the same man being comforted at the side of the car crash.

I knew that the real Leo was inside that sick and inebriated person, and that now was the time for him to begin to come out.

I saw the Spiritual through the pain.

The moment of seeing was now.

The moment of healing could begin.

The moment of miracle was given.

This moment is crucial to my recovery.

Crucial to my understanding of the disease.

Crucial to my thinking about treatment.

For years, people had said I drank too much. For years, people had tried to make me see. Make me understand. Make me face up to myself. They tried to force me into accepting my sickness. My allergy. My disease.

On most occasions, I would mouth verbal abuse or implausible excuses. But now I was seeing it. Seeing me.

And instantly, I moved from "seeing" to "saying"—"I am an alcoholic."

I was admitting to myself that I was an alcoholic. For me, that was—and still is—a cherished miracle.

In England, we have the phrases, "The penny dropped", or "the ice broke", which are used to describe moments when the truth collides with life, and the human being is given a personal and undeniable insight into reality.

For the first time, you actually know.

I mean, *know* know!

I had looked many times, but now I was seeing.

I had listened many times, but now I was hearing.

A point of awareness was reached, and I was involved with reality.

It is frightening.

It is tremendous.

It is true.

When I saw and tasted my disease, I experienced my recovery.

In the facing up,

in the confrontation,

in the encounter with the disease . . . I grasped my recovery.

When I read I Corinthians, it speaks of my moment of awareness.

> *When I was a child, my speech, feelings, and thinking were all those of a child.*
>
> *Now that I am a man, I have no more use for childish ways.*

What we see now is like a dim image in a mirror;
then we shall see face-to-face.
What I know now is only partial;
Then it will be complete—as complete
as God's knowledge of me.[1]

In this passage I am made to see I can walk on water. "Leo, you are an alcoholic."

"Leo, you are an alcoholic." So said the voices within.

I agreed.

As I write these words, I feel the past emotions welling up to the surface. I am so grateful.

I know something about me.

Something true.

Something real.

Something as descriptive as the color of my eyes.

This I needed to know.

A discovery was made that enabled me to open the door to a new life. From the car crash, I discovered something about me. I now had an awareness of me that was real. I had a cherished moment when I said what I secretly knew: "I am an alcoholic."

In that moment, something spiritual was realized.

That given Spirituality was perceived and discovered. I was walking on water.

It is like knowing the feelings of love. When two people are in love, they have strong feelings for each other, excitement, anxiety, joy, vulnerability, need. In such emotions, the real self is experienced. You are in touch with the real you. You know something about yourself. Love is spiritual because it is true. It makes you feel. Love makes you more real.

Another example might be seen in the child who has struggled with a geometry problem for days, and then inexplicably everything fits into place.

A moment of clarity is reached.

You see beyond the equations.

The answer screams at you.

A problem is solved when the problem is seen in its entirety. The solution is in the problem. The recovery is in the pain. Such is the moment.

Another insight might be seen in the Biblical statement at the beginning of Genesis:

Then God commanded, "Let the water below the sky come together in one place, so that the land will appear" — and it was done. He named the land Earth, and the water which had come together He named Sea. And God was pleased with what He saw. Then He commanded: "Let the earth produce all kinds of plants, those that bear grain and those that bear fruit" — and it was done.

So the earth produced all kinds of plants, and God was pleased with what He saw. [2]

These wonderful words only take on meaning, only become real, when you see the beauty of nature. Experience the green trees, rippling streams and warm winds. God's beauty is recognized in His creation. God is to be seen in the mountains or the forest. In the awesome power and mysterious depths of the ocean is God's majesty perceived. God's portrait is in His creation. Our world.

We must feel through these inadequate words to understand this. Words are but the bridges toward reality.

In the energetic birth of a human being eager for life, God's creativity is seen. The baby's first cry is nature's resounding "yes" to God.

God must be seen in the given.
In the flesh and blood of life.
In the beauty and energy of nature.

God's moments are many and various, yet so often we miss them. We miss them because we miss ourselves. So long as we persist in seeking God "out there", so we will miss the miracle of the given.

The miracle of the ordinary.
The bald man sharing his lunch with the sparrows.
The mother duck teaching the ducklings to swim.
The thrill of jogging in the rain.

These are the given miracles of life.

We miss the Divine, because we look for magic. Vincent Van Gogh said, "to put that radiance into human beings that was expressed by the old halos." Being human is a miracle.

My moment after the car crash was a miracle because it put me in touch with who I am.

It enabled me to see something that I needed to see.
Needed to know.
It took me deeper into myself.
Home.
The place where I must live.
This is not only true for the alcoholic. It is true for everybody.
Life,
experiencing life,
feeling life is the contact point that enables us to discover
who we are.
In the understanding of my history is my future.

Everyone has moments when the writing is on the wall. We see it in our lives. We ignore it at our peril.

Incidentally, I am sure that I had other moments before the car crash that revealed my alcoholism, my disease, my compulsive and obsessive behavior, but I denied or ignored them. Not ready. Out for lunch.

The God of Truth has created a world of moments, but there must be a willingness on our part to want to see them.
God is the continuous moment...
But I have to want it.
See it.
Grasp it.

I have to willingly want my recovery. In this sense, Truth is personal.

Using that popular American phrase, the day I grasped my recovery is the moment "I went for it."
I did something terrific for me.
I went for me.

God did not try that day more than any other. God did not think: "Let's force Leo into acceptance."
"Let me make a horrid car crash for Leo when he is drunk."
Such a God would be in need of treatment!

God was always caring for me and loving me, even in my worst moments. Whether I am a vomiting drunk or a recovering priest, God's love is the same. God's love is constant for all His creatures. God loves. Period.

It is not a case of God loving more or less, depending on His temperament that given day. Still less is God's love proportionate to our success. Rather, it was that I cooperated with His Will for me when I made a move for my recovery. I made a move to help me. I began the slow process of loving me back to health. I created the moment by responding to the moment. The freedom of choice creates the moment. Indeed, in the gift of freedom is the miracle.

Not only did I respond at the time of the car crash, but to this day I have chosen to keep that moment alive. When I choose to remember my last drunk, I respond to God's constant Love responsibly.

I continue to cooperate with the miracle.

    I keep the miracle alive.

        I make the miracle happen today.

        I keep the moment alive.

To quote the famous Christian mystic, Simone Weil, "Our consent is necessary in order that God may perform His own creation through us."

        When I know this, I am walking on water.

The alcoholic's disease is not the bottle of alcohol.

The drug addict's problem is not in the syringe.

The over-eater's compulsion does not exist in the fridge.

Las Vegas is not the real enemy of the gambler.

The disease of addiction and obsession lives within the human being. In our feelings and emotions of utter isolation hides the disease.

Those people who are aware of the symptoms of the disease in their own lives, those who are recovering a day at a time, those who by marriage or birth are in a relationship with the disease and have a program of recovery, such people are capable of understanding and giving helpful advice. From their own personal experience, they see the disease's "cunning and baffling" characteristics. They can pull its cover.

Those alcoholics who have only recently discovered they have the disease are wise to listen to those who have been clean and sober for some years. It is common sense to seek the support of those who are sober, living comfortably and serenely a day at a time with the disease. I realize that nobody is the same, and everybody's life has different aspects and characteristics, but the disease of alcoholism, the disease of addiction, has identifiably common symptoms. Just like flu for the Englishman in London has common symptoms that require the same treatment as for the Filipino in Manila, so the symptoms for alcoholism, drug addiction, compulsive eating or gambling are identifiable to all sufferers.

Incidentally, the recovery also has identifiable characteristics! It is not sensible to arrogantly go your own way when it is clashingly different from the experience of the recovering community around you. I have described how the moment of my accepting the disease was and is tremendously important for my growth as a person; however, that growth has been sustained within the recovering community. In the common sharing of my disease with recovering people I am able to use yesterday's horror stories to recharge a positive and creative lifestyle today. Listening to how other people grow and live with their alcoholism helps me to live with mine. This is not only true for the alcoholic, but for all who live with a compulsive and obsessive disease.

The moment the person with an eating disorder is willing to accept that he/she has a disease and needs help is the moment when healing and recovery can begin. The disease should not be seen in the food, but in the destructive attitudes at work in the person's lifestyle. We can discuss our true feelings only when we feel it is okay to own our feelings.

Okay to say who we are.

Okay to say what we feel.

Remember, the disease of compulsion and obsession lives on fear,

loneliness,

anger,

hatred,

denial,

guilt,

self-pity.

A symptom of the disease is seen in the power we have taken from ourselves and given to others. The disease thrives when it gets us to mistreat and abuse ourselves. It first works on getting us to dislike ourselves, and then grows stronger in our unhappiness. It gives us false messages about what we look like,

critical messages about our ethnic background,

the color of our skin,

our sexual orientation.

These messages combine to make us unhappy with our life situation. Reality becomes too painful to live with. We need to escape.

We eat.

Eat ourselves out of reality.

Eat ourselves into fantasy.

We deny ourselves any creative and balanced pleasure for an indulgence in food that only makes us feel sick, sad and guilty.

Then we vomit, we purge ourselves. The vicious cycle is triggered. We feel self-pity and bad because we eat, and yet our disease tells us the only comfort and satisfaction we get in life comes from eating.

We eat on anger,
depression,
lack of sex,
loneliness,
fear,
isolation.

The key to recovery is Spirituality.

Spirituality is in seeing,
appreciating,
recognizing the beauty that exists within.

We must love beyond the fatness into our real selves. We must force the honesty through the layers of fat flesh in order to realize and appreciate the beautiful person within. If we have a poor opinion of ourselves, if we do not think we are of much value, if we are unable to see any positive features in our lives, then it is not surprising that we are destroying ourselves.

If we behaved on the road like we behave in our lives, we would be considered suicidal. The pain and chaos in our lives are shouts for help.

A silent shout,
A secret shout,
A hidden shout.

Help comes when the individual hears his own cry. Recovery is available if the person really wants it,

is prepared to ask for it,
will work for it.

Using the analogy of the drowning man, unless he shouts, he cannot be rescued. Unless he lets go of the rock that is pulling him down, he will not survive. However, he must make the first move. He must let go.

People who have problems with drugs, alcohol, gambling, food, or any situation that is out of control will be able to identify with the above feelings, and in order for recovery to happen, the person concerned must make a move.

I do not mean that we cannot get help from other people or self-help groups, but nobody can help until we make some kind of positive response to our pain. That is why the "moment" is so important. Having that point in our lives when we can see and hear the truth.

I mean *really* see.

Really hear.

Really understand what is happening in our lives.

This is the moment we walk on water.

When we perceive that the disease of unmanageability and powerlessness exists within our personal lives.

When we see that we need to take responsibility for our disease. Take responsibility for our daily actions. Take responsibility for our attitudes.

Once we see the need to take responsibility for the disease that is ruining our lives, we begin the moment of recovery.

As with all diseases, the symptoms are clear to those with eyes to see and ears to hear. The symptoms need to be "shouted out" for the sufferer to hear. It is often therapeutically beneficial to get the sufferer, the patient, to "shout out" his symptoms. Shout them out so that the experience brings its own personal perceptions. I deliberately use the word "shout" because that point of urgency and pain must be reached before the sufferer can hear his need.

In the screamed shout are the symptoms expressed.

The fear,

loneliness,

depression,

anger,

resentments,

apathy,

tiredness,

confusion,

insanity,

faithlessness,

hatred,

rage,

sadness,

aggression,

impotence,

annoyance.

Also, the broken relationships,

physical violence,

unemployment,

poor physical health,

dangerously low self-esteem.

Then add police convictions,
    treatment in mental hospitals,
        suicide attempts.
The life of an addict is a life of torments. A personal torture chamber that is self-inflicted.
    It is like the victim giving sticks to the mugger. As he cringes, he says, "Hit me." Until this insanity is seen, the disease will always win.
    Rigorous honesty,
        pulling the cover on yourself,
            seeing the lies and manipulations that feed the
                compulsive and obsessive behavior is the treatment
                    that must become the lifestyle.
Many who have gone through treatment call their life a Program. A daily spiritual orientation. An altered lifestyle that they have chosen. The disease is arrested by the honest decision you choose to make concerning your life.
    Deciding to be honest,
        to live in the now,
            to live a day at a time,
                when in the wrong to admit it,
                    learn to forgive and ask forgiveness,
                        seeking God in all aspects of your life.
This is how we continue to discover who we are. Who we are is what we have to live with.
    When I begin to love myself, I begin to love God and God's world.
    When I hate myself, I miss God and His world.
    You begin to love yourself when you begin to know yourself:
                "Physician, heal thyself."
God is involved in your treatment, but so are you. Your cooperation in treatment is Divine. That part of God that is you must be involved in recovery.
                This is the miracle of walking on water.
    Needless to say, I see all of these as aspects of the giveness of Spirituality.
    The discovery of who you are and what you have is Spiritual.
    It is positive and creative and with it we build bridges to other human beings in need. In the shared suffering of the recovering addict with the suffering addict is the miracle of healing given.
    This great adventure turns out to be the only adventure worth taking for any human being: the journey into self.

So I return to that crazy journey that led to the car crash. You remember, I did not make it home. Now I can see that it was impossible for me to ever arrive "home" by going that route. Even if I had parked the car in the garage, entered the house and closed the door for the night, clumsily undressed and got into bed, I would still have been a long way from home. The birth of my disease began with the journey away from me; fed, encouraged and supported by my alcoholic drinking, my addiction. That place in me that prefers fantasy to reality is where my disease lives. For years, it was camouflaged and hidden by my poor self-esteem and guilty feelings. The alcohol took me further and further away from me, and at the time of my car crash I was a long way from home. I was years away from where I was meant to be. The physical car crash made this clear. I saw what was happening to my life. This is why that moment is so special and important to me today. It proved to be the point at which I started to go home.

Go home to me.

I caught a glimpse of the real me, and I wanted him back.

When I saw the film *E.T.*, I was made to see my life and my addiction more clearly. Like E.T., I had accidentally entered the wrong world and I could not survive in that world. The drinking world was not where I was meant to be. I was not physically equipped to drink alcohol.

E.T. needed to "go home" to live.

I needed to go home to the reality of his alcoholism in order to survive. To be comfortable in my world, I needed to go home to reality. The choice was mine.

Choice is part of my story.

It still is.

The young boy in *E.T.* also had a choice. Was he to stay home with his family or go to another world with E.T.? He chose to stay in his real world.

I needed to make a choice to discover the real me. Saying I was an alcoholic was just the beginning—I must now live with my choice, live with my disease.

Life is a series of moments. All are special, but some stand out. I thank God for the moment I knew what for years others had said:

"I am an alcoholic."

I am glad I know it.

I do not like my alcoholism, but I have grown to love it—
because it is an important part of me.

What about you?

[1] I Corinthians 13:11.
[2] Genesis 1:9-12.

5 | TWO HEADS

Historically, man has often seen himself in the middle of a supernatural battle. The forces of light against the forces of darkness. Evil trying to destroy Truth. Satan seeking power in God's world.

Holy Books recount it. Religions immortalize it. Dante's *Inferno* endeavors to describe it.

It is not just a Biblical theme. Modern man is still preoccupied with it. Superman stands for truth against the various gangsters of terror. Batman and Robin encounter every danger to stop the "dastardly deeds" of the pernicious Penguin! Nowhere is this seen more clearly than in the epic drama of *Star Wars*. In the saga, a small but noble force of the Jedi is fighting the terrifying legions of the Empire, led by the evil ex-Jedi, Darth Vader.

Such dramas feed our imaginations. They reflect some of our fears. They expose our inner aspirations. We all feel part of a great drama. At times, we all believe in Destiny, consider Fate, consult the stars. We then laugh and say it is nonsense . . . but we wonder.

I want to bring this supernatural battle into our own lives.

I know when I get angry with something, it is because it has caught me, touched me, troubled me in some way. I cry in a movie because the drama is within me. I am enthused at the victory of another human being because of the personal victories I have faced in me. I know me.

In a wonderful TV drama, "Playing for Time," an argument develops between the Jewish and Polish women who make up the orchestra for the Nazi Concentration Camp. One Polish prisoner, describing the camp guards, screams, "They are animals."

The Jewish heroine replies, "That is just the point . . . They are not animals. If they were animals, we should expect what is happening. The tragedy is that they are human beings. Men and women like you and me. It is human beings who are doing these things to us!"

When I am experiencing this kind of drama, I get in touch with that noble side of me that cries against the injustice.

Weeps at the waste.

Feels sick in the shame.

Yet this same experience reveals the brutal Nazi in me. That side of Leo that likes the boots and uniform. That side of me that sees the pain and enjoys it.

Sees the power and wants it.

That is the truth.

I have always tried to hide that side of me, now I own it.

If I watch a rape scene,

I am horrified.

Disgusted at being human.

Revolted at the forced intimacy.

Yet, at the same time, the experience reveals a side of me that seeks the fantasy. Enjoys the fighting, force, pain, and excitement. Revels in the sexual violence. That is the truth.

I have two sides of me. Two heads. All human beings have two heads. A sick head and a healthy head. We actually have seventy times seven heads, but two will make the point!

There is a side of us that wants to achieve,

be somebody,

make it in life.

However, the other head tells us we are no good, stupid and unworthy. Many of us cannot accept a compliment because of what the sick head is saying. "You are no good." It is the drama of the sick and healthy going on within. The conflict of light and darkness. It is being an angel in the dirt.

It is the Jekyl and Hyde syndrome. Inside is the monster . . . the destructive . . . the diseased . . . the cruel. Most times he is kept under control, but at times he breaks out.

He looks like me.

Talks like me.

Walks like me.
  He is a part of me.
    That dark side of me.
      That hidden me.
        That imperfect me.
          He is the part of me that needs healing.
            The attitude that needs changing.
              The ego in me that needs humility.
I am not perfect. I will never be perfect. Yet, I must try to be better. I must manage my Mr. Hyde.

In the early part of my story, *Dr. Jekyl and Mr. Hyde,* we see that Dr. Jekyl did appear to control the appearances of Mr. Hyde. Mr. Hyde only came out when Dr. Jekyl took the drug. For years, Dr. Jekyl lived his life as a sensitive and caring doctor. Then he decided to reveal his darker side. The evil within. He took a drug that manifested Mr. Hyde. For a while things were fine. Dr. Jekyl semed to be in control. Then one day, one horrid day, the day with which all addicts can identify, the thin line was crossed. A strange and destructive "moment" was realized — Mr. Hyde appeared in Dr. Jekyl's life without being invited. The power struggle had begun. To the complete astonishment of Dr. Jekyl, Mr. Hyde had been quietly and unobtrusively developing strength. Mr. Hyde was the progressive disease. He was now ready for the take over. Mr. Hyde was in control.

A vivid illustration of the two heads. Mr. Hyde represents the disease. He progressed in strength without the drug, and existed in the emotions and feelings of Dr. Jekyl. Then that moment in the life of the disease is reached when the line is crossed between abuse and addiction.

The tail is now wagging the dog; indeed, the tail is the dog!

Every alcoholic knows this moment. Every drug addict lives this experience. Every gambler can remember. Things are not going as expected. Something is wrong. This moment could take a period of months or years to come into effect, but the shift of power is real.

The choices we make in our lives awaken the disease; the disease feeds on the crazy decisions and insane behavior patterns we live out.

The two heads come into conflict. The diseased head is growing in strength. Our sick actions only make him stronger.

How do we take Mr. Hyde's power away?

Two Heads

By seeing what is happening. Altering attitudes. Changing direction. Seeking professional help to change our sick lifestyle. Involving ourselves in Alcoholics Anonymous or a similar program. Domestically moving away from our temptations. Considering the dangers in our employment. Evaluating the kind of friendships we have. Locating the survivors with our disease and joining them. Living one day at a time in the right attitude.

Accepting there is no "cure", but only daily growth. A constant battle with our sick head that brings its own rewards.

Acknowledging aloud that we want recovery more than anything else. That the disease of obsession and compulsion is the prime problem. That we have become the problem. It is within us. Exaggerating the point, "My disease is Leo. I am an alcoholic."

The millions of people in therapy know this is true. On the way to the therapist, your sick head says:

"You don't need to see him."

"You are better now."

"Other people have problems without rushing to see a shrink."

"No wonder he smiles at you. Your fees have bought him a new car."

"If you were getting better, you wouldn't need him."

The healthy head tells you not to listen. Remembers the pain that existed before therapy. Tells you to trust the therapist and his directions. Reminds you of the many joys in daily recovery.

Recovering alcoholics meet the sick head every day. He is "cunning, baffling, and powerful".[1]

He says, "You don't need a meeting tonight."

"Take the young chick out for a ride instead of listening to dreary oldtimers."

"Stay in, read a good book, and pour yourself just one little gin."

"All this talk about alcoholism will drive you back to alcohol."

It is not only alcoholics or those in therapy who have two heads. In any argument, in any home, the heads are battling.

"I will not say I'm sorry until he says he's sorry."

"So they think I'm a child. I'll show them what being irresponsible is. They'll be sorry."

"I don't know why I married a fool like you.

Everybody said you were no good."

"I wish you were dead."

Then, after we have banged the door and calmed down, we ask ourselves, "Did I say all that? Whatever made me say those cruel things?"

Sometimes the sick head leads to action. The wife is crying and the husband is bleeding. The child trembles with fear as the door opens. The paramedics take the body away. Darkness. Evil. And it is all within.

The therapy comes in knowing that the battle is going on. Everybody gets crazy moments. Everybody feels like running away or hitting the boss. All children say insensitive things to their parents. All parents say insensitive things to their children. It is part of being imperfect. Being human. Not being God. However, when the destructive voices lead to destructive behavior, seek help.

This was the point of my sharing my moment with you. For years, I had listened to my alcoholic head saying to the world, "Screw you. I want to drink." For years I listened to my crazy "IC". He promised he would take my difference away. Remove my loneliness and fear. Take my shame away. For years, I believed that crazy and insane "IC". Then I stopped still and saw me. I had a moment of sanity. Knew his game. Saw my sickness. Accepted my alcoholism.

I had treatment for my alcoholism in a hospital. They explained the background of my two heads—and they told me I was not alone. I WAS NOT ALONE. This I needed to hear. I was not the only one in the world who had a voice that said in the hotel bar, "Now leave this drink with your company, excuse yourself and go to the toilet, on your way order a large gin and drink it before you return . . . clever boy."

In hospital therapy groups, I discovered that all the patients had similar messages and I knew I belonged. From the aged chief to the unmarried Polish girl, the pain and sufferings were the same, only the locations were different. Know your "IC". In the hospital, I started to face my disease and began growing up.

This is walking on water.

Walking on water is knowing that all human beings get crazy now and then. The miracle happened when I could talk about my crazy head. The miracle grew when other people shared their sick heads.

We become human when we share our humanness. Share our two heads. This is reality.

With widespread dishonesty and people-pleasing, nobody knows what reality is anymore. People miss what being human really is. We cannot love our neighbors because we do not know them. Few know their families and friends.

How many of us have honest conversations?

How many share our fears?

Can we be ourselves?

We get exhausted hiding. Hence the doctor bills. The sedatives. The prescription drugs. The crates of alcohol. The eating binges. The suicide attempts. The Great Lie.

This constant game-playing leads us into the negative force. It takes us to the power of darkness. The dishonesty and denial keep us prisoners of the Cosmic Disease that all religions and cultures speak about.

However, we have the power of choice.

The ability to cooperate with truth.

The God-given gift of freedom.

We do not have to remain sick. We do not have to remain dishonest. We can choose the creative force. The healthy head. We are creative creatures, not conditioned robots. Herein is the miracle of Spirituality.

To know the Nazi in me is not to be the Nazi.

To know the rapist in me is not to be the rapist.

To know the sick head is not to live the sick head.

When I was a child, I asked my mother, "How do I become a prince?" Mother said, "By thinking noble thoughts." I still believe that. You become a prince when you think noble and lofty thoughts. Martin Luther King and Albert Schweitzer were princes, not because they lived in castles or dressed in fine linen, but because they dared to dream. They lived their dreams. They dared others to dream.

Their greatness included their crazyness.

They learned to live with their two heads.

They accepted the gift of Spirituality from God and dared to risk. They died saying "yes" to Life.

We choose the forces in life we want. That is the miracle of being a free human being. You follow the head you choose. At the end of the day, a human being does what he wants to do.

You make your world.

You bring into your world what you are choosing.

If you choose a noble life, you will seek out noble friends.

If you choose a dishonest life, you will seek dishonest friends.

The chosen force within radiates and attracts.

Creative periods in history have themselves produced the noblest aspirations of men, the finest craftsmanship, and most spiritual prophets. The dark periods of history stank to Heaven with cruelty, insanity and mediocrity. Human beings did it all.

In order to make my world Spiritual, I must develop and contribute my creativity and my positiveness.

Knowing the existence of my two heads is sanity.

<hr />

[1] *The Big Book,* Alcoholics Anonymous.

SURRENDER TO LIVE

A little Jewish girl in Germany in 1937, told her school teacher that her cat had given birth to five kittens, so very beautiful kittens, and "they are all darling little Nazis." A month later, an official of the German propaganda ministry visited the school, and the teacher asked her to repeat her story.

"Yes, Herr Inspector," she said, "my cat gave birth to five beautiful kittens and they are all darling little Social Democrats." "What," shouted the teacher, "I thought you told me they were darling little Nazis?" "Oh yes, they were," replied the little girl, "but that was four weeks ago. Now their eyes are open."

The key to the understanding of Spirituality is seeing ourselves. Seeing what is happening behind the smile,
behind the "I feel fine,"
behind the mask.

Spirituality is not "out there". It does not come with negative self-denial, religious laws or bodily sacrifices that can so easily feed the ego. Spirituality is in being real.

Spirituality reflects the Power that God has given every one of us.

Spirituality stops your waiting for a miracle,
looking for a miracle,
asking for a miracle.

Spirituality reminds you that YOU ARE THE MIRACLE. The spark of the Divine is in Elsie, Harold and Moses. Spirituality gives achievement and dignity to your body, mind and emotions, by telling you to "go for it". Everything that God created belongs to you, and you belong to it. Knowing this is walking on water.

Such power involves an element of risk. We can screw it up. We can hide. We can seek escape in the various forms of addiction. We can live and act as if our lives are worthless. We can choose a form of slavery in people-pleasing. We can hide behind food or religion. We can remain sick behind the mask of prejudice and false piety. Be prim, proper and in pain.

On the other hand, Spirituality is . . .

discovering reality,
saying no to fantasy,
being real.

The word "hypocrite" comes from a Greek word meaning, "one who wears a mask".

In the ancient Greek Theatre, a mask was worn by actors to portray different characters and emotions. If you were the villain, you would wear an evil-looking mask; the hero, a handsome mask; and so on. They had masks for all the feelings: anger, fear, terror, joy and happiness.

The mask was used to act out a part. Be somebody else. Reveal an unfelt feeling. In any one play, an actor could wear many masks. Today, in modern theatre, we paint on a face. Use special effects to bring about an illusion. Utilize lighting and music to produce an emotion. Such is Drama.

In real life, the element of fantasy can be dangerous. We can so easily avoid the symptoms of our disease or discomfort by seeking escape in "fantasy", and in this manipulated dishonesty the disease grows in strength.

We choose to avoid what is happening within us.

We prefer illusion.

We live in the trick.

We make a choice for addiction.

We may go to work, get married, pay mortgages, have children, receive promotions, sing in Church, and appear "fine;" but inside we are dying.

We have not faced Reality.
We have chosen Fantasy.
We have not Surrendered.

Surrender. An interesting word. How many people would connect the word surrender with Spirituality? However, without Surrender there can be no perceived Spirituality. Interestingly enough, the word Islam means "to surrender." The word Muslim means "one who has surrendered."

The Prophet Mohammed was concerned about the behavior of his followers when they drank alcohol, and so he decided to tell them to stop drinking for a period of time before and after fixed religious prayers. The fixed prayer was several times a day. However, this did not stop the drunkenness. During the free times, many of the Arabs got drunk, becoming cruel and hostile. It was at this point that The Prophet forbade the use of alcohol. No Muslim should drink alcohol. They should "surrender" to a higher rule; the rule of God. Hence, the abstinence practiced in many Muslim countries.

Occasionally, Christian sects and other religious groups have abstained from alcohol in order to attain a more productive and spiritual lifestyle; however, abstinence from alcohol is not a part of the Christian tradition.

Surrender follows "the moment" you open your eyes to the real you. Really see the dynamics of a disease in your life, recognize obsessive behavior, catch the insanity in your life.

Is your marriage working?
Are you drinking too much?
Is your gambling causing problems?
How many cigarettes are you smoking, and can you breathe in the morning?
Do you eat too much?
Is your religion a means of avoiding life?
Are you sick and in need of help?

Surrender to the reality of your life. Put aside the fancy talk and lies. Be real. Surrender.

Imagine the scene: I am a young soldier in Colonel John Wayne's Calvary Troop. We have gone some miles from Fort Apache, and suddenly we are attacked by thousands of screaming Indians. We form a circle at the Colonel's command and begin to defend ourselves. More Indians are coming over the hills.

I am afraid. We are powerless over our predicament and our concentration has become unmanageable.

I look at the Colonel. He looks fierce and is fighting. Still the Indians attack.

More troops are being killed. I am still afraid.

I look at the Colonel again. He still looks fierce and is fighting. In a whisper, I ask, "Do you think we should surrender?"

I knew I should have waited for a more appropriate time to speak to the Colonel! He shouts, "So long as the flag is flying, we will be fighting." At that moment, Sergeant Muggins, whose job it was to hold high the flag, falls to the ground with several arrows in his chest. He looks awfully dead.

More Indians pour over the hills.

Our situation is becoming more serious by the minute. Only the Colonel, a young soldier called Charles, and I are left. Finally, Charles gets hit in a secret place.

I look at the Colonel. He looks at me.

"Shall we consider surrender?" I say, at a quiet moment.

"Americans do not surrender!" he exclaims.

I say quickly, "I'm English . . . we always surrender."

This seems to reassure him. He reluctantly agrees to surrender. I raise a white handkerchief that I keep for such occasions, and we surrender to live.

WE SURRENDERED TO LIVE. The message from this crazy story is people surrender to live!

The word surrender, which in my drinking days I always connected with weak and negative people, is the bridge to a deeper understanding of me. It is essential for spiritual growth. When the alcoholic accepts his alcoholism, he surrenders to this reality—to the painful, but life-giving fact that his drinking is never going to be social, and that he will never have complete control over it. The miracle is finding a way to live with the disease.

So I return to my central point: people surrender to live. In the history of mankind, nobody has surrendered to die! In a very real way, surrender is not cowardice, but common sense. It is facing the facts, taking all the aspects of the situation into consideration, and making a decision—a decision to survive.

The use of the word surrender infers that there has been some fight, some conflict, some pain—and recovery begins when it is realized we cannot win this way. By stopping the battle, we achieve the victory. Hence, we surrender to live.

The truth is that every alcoholic has been a valiant fighter with his disease for years. He tried to cut down his drinking, change his brand of drinks, limit his drinking to the weekends—in short, he tried everything to be like a social drinker — but because he has a disease, he could never succeed. He is not to blame for being an alcoholic. He did not intend to have these problems. People are never ambitious for alcoholism.

What do I mean by a disease? A deep rooted un-ease, uncomfortability, un-connectedness. A feeling of being not-centered, a quiet falling apart . . . a sickness that affects every fibre of our humanity. It is a disease, for God's Sake! In the same way that epilepsy, diabetes and hyperglycemia are diseases, so is alcoholism. If anything, the emphasis should be on the alcoholic taking responsibility for his disease, rather than feeling responsible for having it! Ignorant people, religious and medical, who persist in fostering guilt only add insult to injury and become the social symptoms of this disease.

Ignorance has always been the obstacle to healing. For this reason, I maintain that the alcoholic who surrenders to the facts of his disease is neither a coward nor weak-willed, but courageous and realistic. To see things as they are, rather than how we would like them to be, is the discovery of Spirituality.

It is suicide to continue fighting when you have no chance of victory—or when the writing is on the wall, we do well to heed it. Surrender to the reality and live. That is walking on water.

This book is filled with such moments. Times when we, nobody else, must make a decision.

> The choice is often life or death,
>   destruction or creativity,
>   health or disease,
>   recovery or continued pain.

An ultimate tragedy is promised in a foolish choice.

The decision to have that first drink.

A bottle of booze left in the fridge.

An evening spent in the wrong company, instead of going to an A.A. meeting.

The journey toward pain and death started in that foolish choice. The whispered "yes" that should have been "no". We all have such moments of decision.

I stopped fighting alcohol because I could not win. God knows I had tried. The arguments, the police arrests, the geographical moves, the humiliations are there to see.

The pain, the loneliness, the fear, the anger can still be felt. Alcohol always brought me problems. I never went into battle with booze and won.

Surrender To Live

$$2 + 2 = 4$$

Leo + Alcohol = Problems.

Just as 2 + 2 is always 4, so Leo + alcohol is always trouble.

The moment of sanity came when I saw it. When I recognized it. When I surrendered to live.

The story of me and Colonel Wayne explains our resistance to the idea of Surrender. We want to be seen as powerful. In control. In charge. Everything working for us. Nothing must be seen as weak. Nothing vulnerable. Nothing chaotic. Winning is everything. Macho men . . . playing God.

Remember, the sin of Adam was wanting to be "as God". The Devil tempted Adam and Eve with the fruit of the tree that would enable them to be "like God". Pride. The oldest sin.

Pride.

The fertile foundation for any addiction.

To be like God.

> *Now the snake was the most cunning animal that the Lord God had made. The snake asked the woman, "Did God really tell you not to eat fruit from any tree in the garden?"*
>
> *"We may eat the fruit of any tree in the garden," the woman answered, "except the tree in the middle of it. God told us not to eat the fruit of that tree, or even touch it; if we do, we will die."*
>
> *The snake replied, "That's not true; you will not die."[1]*

In Colonel Wayne, we see our people-pleasing. Miles away from anywhere, the Colonel is still trying to impress the General, or his father, or somebody. His pride takes him to the edge of the abyss. His suicidal attempt can be seen in his stubborn battle against overwhelming odds.

In countless wars, over many generations, thousands of men have died because a few men chose to impress their General. Ego is the real enemy. I have a fantasy that while the Colonel and I are knee-deep in Indians, the General back at Fort Apache is busy eating sprouts and planning a vacation. The General is taking care of himself. That is sanity.

I remember during my drinking days wanting to drink like a man—I had long since given up the idea of drinking like a gentleman! However, I always ended up drinking like a lush. Drinking like a drunk. For years, mixing ego with alcohol, I continued to try to drink like a man. Crazy. I imagined people wanted me to drink like a man. Crazy. I thought people were preoccupied with watching me. Crazy.

I suppose the people I was trying to impress were like the General, they were busy eating sprouts and planning vacations. Living ordinary lives. Sanity. I remember when I stopped drinking for a time I hated myself. I was ashamed of my inability to drink like other people. I was angry, resentful, bitter, and full of self-pity. This was my brief period of dryness. Dryness is not sobriety. Although I was not drinking, I had not accepted my alcoholism . . . then the moment of acceptance came after a car crash. I not only accepted my alcoholism, I accepted myself. I faced reality in my life. I realized there were other things that I could not do successfully.

I am not a musician, painter, skater, chess player, mountaineer, sailor or mechanic. The list could go on. There are things that I can do, and there are things that I cannot do. That is life. That is my life.

Is it such a big deal that I cannot drink alcohol successfully? Is it? This I can live with.

Of course, every now and again I can return to my "oh so personal" pity pot.

> "Life was unfair."
> "Misery, I know thee well."
> "Fancy God doing such a thing to me."

Early in my recovery, I remember thinking that if I became a Roman Catholic priest, the curse of alcoholism might be removed from my life. Then I thought about the Roman Catholic priests I knew, and the idea immediately vanished. I never did get around to thinking about being a Rabbi!

From this self-indulgent prison, I began to see the real world. I saw children accepting their blindness. Crippled youths struggling to play in sports. The blind learning the piano. I saw my mother taking her tablet for angina. My father enjoying growing old. I was so preoccupied with what I thought was being taken away from me that I did not recognize what I was given.

I was drowning in self-pity, because I would not let go of the Rock of Resentment.

It was only when I was prepared to let go of the unreal perception of me and my disease that I could recover and begin to live.

When I decided to "let go", I developed gratitude . . . a gratitude that grew with my acceptance of myself. People sometimes ask, "What do you mean by 'let go?' " I mean, talk out the stuff in your life that is unreal. Put out that which is untrue. Reveal and discuss the deceit and manipulation. Throw off the masks that keep us hidden.

You "let go" to be free.

You "let go" to live.

You "let go" to be real.

Gratitude flows from that which is given, rather than from that which is taken. What was taken, we give back. The real we keep.

Now I see that in exchange for alcohol I could have every real facet of life and also feel 100% healthier. The bargain of a lifetime.

Today I accept my compulsive and obsessive disease, and I smile.

I thank God.

I begin to laugh.

Like the kittens, my eyes are opened.

[1]*Good News Bible,* Today's English Version, Genesis 3:1-4.

7

BEING DIFFERENT

Tis true my form is something odd,
But blaming me is blaming God,
Could I create myself anew,
I would not fail in pleasing you.

If I could reach from pole to pole,
Or grasp the ocean with a span,
I would be measured by the soul,
The mind's the standard of a man.

Joseph Merrick, *The Elephant Man*

I wonder if like me you catch the difference in you. Sometimes I am going along the road, and I find myself feeling different from other people, for no apparent reason. I may be at a party, and I begin to feel different. Or I am in a church, around a pool, or alone in a room, when suddenly I feel overwhelmingly different.

It is difficult to describe.

A feeling.

Hard to explain.

But it is there, always there, though I am not always aware of it. Do you feel different at times?

When I express these feelings to my friends who are recovering alcoholics, they usually say it is because I am alcoholic. That I am

71

getting in touch with my compulsive personality, and that my ego is making me feel different. Yet, when I talk with nonalcoholics, they often confide in me their feelings of "difference".

Does this mean that all alcoholics are the same and yet different from nonalcoholics?

Does this mean that the alcoholic is different from other drug addicts, and both are different from nonalcoholics? Are alcoholics the only people with egos? What does it mean to be different?

I do not think I feel different because I am alcoholic. I suspect that we all feel different at times. We all feel "less than" or "more than" at times.

I am going to describe a situation where I would feel different, awkward and uncomfortable. A happening where my difference would make itself felt. My situation for feeling different will be different from your situation, but owning the difference, working through the difference, the acceptance of the difference can be beneficial.

My difference is revealed around alcohol. The difference is not alcohol. The difference is within me. It is me that makes the difference.

I encounter my individuality in my difference.

I encounter my uniqueness in my difference.

In the acceptance of my difference, I am walking on water.

Now it is important for you, as you read, to locate and become aware of your difference. What produces the difference for you will be different, but the feeling will be the same.

It could be food,
being Black,
not being able to write
or alcohol.

What brings out your difference?

One kind of situation in which I feel different and awkward is at a party where large amounts of alcohol are being served. I look at the other guests and I know I feel different from them. I know the reason. I accept the reason. My feeling different has to do with my disease.

I do not act awkward. But I feel awkward. I want to jump on the table and ask the guests not to drink too much. However, I'm a liberal. I believe in freedom. They have a right to a hangover!

I begin to notice the signs of my awkward feelings. I laugh before the joke is over. I'm dropping peanuts on the plant again.

I Do Not Need Alcohol To Live

Inside me, the fear begins to rise. Yesterday's memories crowd into my mind. I begin to notice how the drinker holds his glass and how freely he touches his guest and holds her. My fixed hand around my chin reveals the tension. Most recovering alcoholics feel tense and anxious around people drinking large amounts of alcohol. They are common feelings. My difference is alive and kicking.

The other guests see only a good party emerging. I experience pain and looming disaster. In my mind, I project a fight, a neighbor complaining, and police involvement. These feelings do not arise at every party. Only sometimes.

The drunk has moved to the piano. He has put down his glass. He is eating a cherry and frankfurter. Sickness rumbles within. Another guy is mixing a most odd cocktail. I detect a familiar smell coming from the bathroom. Feelings return. Even the sight of a barman cleaning a glass in a familiar way brings back memories of my difference.

Memories that are connected with pain.

Memories that keep me sober.

Memories of me.

In this sense, I am different. Not different because I have memories and feelings. Different in the kind of memories and feelings I have.

For me, these feelings are the reality and acceptance of my disease. My compulsive and obsessive disease. My Alcoholism. But my disease extends beyond a compulsion with alcohol. Indeed, I catch my compulsive behavior being activated in other situations, not necessarily associated with drinking . . . like gambling in Las Vegas. When I win, I want more. When I lose, I spend more. Always the thrill of winning guides me through the losses. I want it all. Now. In my room afterward, a tired mind replays my mistakes: "If only . . ." "If only I had not done this, if only I had not done that. If only I had stopped when . . ."

Occasionally, my disease of compulsion extends to food and people. I want more of it. More of them. I get thirsty for friends, gluttonous in relationships. All the fears, tensions, resentments and manipulations are involved. I lie in order to fix people, seek to control my calories, eat in my anger, eat after anger, eat away my anger . . . all the things I did around alcohol. The acting, people-pleasing and hiding rise up again. Then I will look up from the table and say, "I feel fine." It's a lie. A painful and sickly lie. My disease is alive and kicking.

I get in touch with my difference in such situations. These situations are not good or bad, better or worse. They simply reveal my difference. My difference is not these situations, not alcohol, food, gambling or relationships. The difference is within me. My sick feelings. They need to be recognized, accepted and confronted.

Why? Because they are real. They are real feelings. They are what is happening in my life. To heal, to recover (a day at a time, because that is all I have), I need to know me. Know all I can of me. Because it is all me. Owning the feeling is the beginning of action. I have made a Spiritual move when I accept what is real. The action, the footwork, the healing touch, can begin when I accept my difference. I encounter my individuality in my difference. I encounter my uniqueness in my difference.

People do not want you to be different. They want you to be the same. The ruling majority want you to accept what they accept,
> believe what they believe,
>> think what they think,
>>> behave like they behave.

Most societies are like this. In this way, they structure, organize, keep control. They want to wield power.

Religion is an institution of society. Religion fears difference. Religion often resists miracles — the spontaneous, original thought which is often where miracles occur. Religion resists miracles except those miracles that work through the power structure. Religion is suspicious and critical of the evolving saint, i.e., examines and scrutinizes the creative or different idea about life. Why? To avoid involving the Church, Tradition, and "God" with the religious crank, the pious fake, the popular charlatan. In its way, Religious Government is trying to remain honorable and pure. Remember not many yesterdays ago, the holder of miracle had the determining power. Unscrupulous people desirous of power would manipulate tricks to indicate Divine acceptance and miracle. Even the honorable and pure mystics were investigated. This was the tragedy of Joan of Arc. Her rigorous honesty and truthfulness would not allow her to be helped into innocent deceit, even when the deceit would give her freedom.

Joan of Arc was being investigated by the Bishop, who was tryng to spare her from being burned at the stake for saying she had heard God's voice. The Bishop said, "Don't you think it could be your imagination?" Joan thought for a moment, and then replied, "Yes, it was my imagination."

The Bishop breathed a sigh of relief. He thought to himself, "Thank God, we can save her from the fires." However, Joan of Arc continued, "It was my imagination because that is the way that God speaks to me."

Joan's difference can be seen in her imagination. In her awareness of God's voice. In her chosenness. To the religious authorities, she was crazy, creepy and demonic. Here we see how the Church's unreal perception of God's activities brought injustice. An unimaginative and predictable awareness of God's varied gifts to mankind brings suffocating conformity.

That is why I argue for a free and diversified appreciation of Spirituality. A Spirituality that is not a prisoner of religion. As we see in Joan of Arc's experience, Spirituality can be revealed in human imagination.

Indeed, the Church can be wrong. Religious attitudes can be wrong. The powerful majority can be wrong.

In the story of Joan, are we not seeing again the trial of Jesus? The condemnation of the different? The crucifixion of God's miracle?

Let us go back to that party. One drunk is still vomiting and the other is still mixing odd cocktails. Little changes at these parties! Now that I own my awkwardness and uncomfortableness, I can leave, go home. I wasn't enjoying it much anyway. Or I can speak to the hostess. Possibly change rooms. Preferably houses! I might even divulge information to the heavy drinkers. "You know, I used to drink like you . . ." Unlikely.

Alternatively my difference could hook me into the disease. I could "drink in" the situation. By this, I mean enjoy their drinking too much. Linger over the drinks. Be fascinated by the bottles, the ice, the floating lemon. Even the anger, resentments, feelings of repulsion could be a set-up. Part of the fantasy. I would be judge and victim. I would be choosing to stay in the sickness — to condemn the sickness! Remain with the drug that makes me feel uncomfortable, stay where the disease is active.

I can choose to enable or to rescue. Both are sick. I can set standards. Do peoples' inventories. Play God. Pronounce forgiveness. Seek a penance. Offer a solution. Secretly enjoy my sickness and pretend it is recovery.

I could want a drink. Not have a drink, but want a drink. Want the fantasy back. Seek the attention. Experience third-hand the drug of escape. Begin to feel carefree. Irresponsible. Slightly envious of the drinker's fun.

Occasionally, I experience these feelings, especially at a party where I have a ready audience, where there is the desire to please people. Enjoy the trap of compliments. Excuse the acceptance of a lethal drink because it was bad manners to refuse. Delusion, lies and pretense. Even if you placed the gin and Coke immediately on the next table, the fires of doom burn closely. Next time . . . To please people we hardly know, we play a dangerous game. The disease makes its presence felt, and the difference is not felt too keenly.

Every addict knows the lines. Those who have not experienced the hell of addiction make the same inane remarks for every obsession. "Everyone drinks beer. Beer can't harm you. Don't let me drink alone."

"Just have some of this ice cream with me. You old party-pooper."

"A little gambling never hurt anybody. Who ever goes to Las Vegas to swim?"

"If you loved me, you would do what I ask you. Don't you love me anymore?"

In every home, in every office, in every school the temptations to do what others want are served up in a variety of ways, all carrying their own special and subtle guilt-trip if refused. The message is always the same: Be what others want. Say what the crowd wants to hear. Sell your soul for the quick applause.

We are told not to be different. Society does not accept those who are different. God disapproves of the different. The Bible rejects the different. The Church often condemns the different.

We are told that to be different is to die alone. Most believe what they are told. It is easier to join the crowd than explain or fight the criticism. Anything for an easy life.

But is it easy? What about the fight going on within!

In some respects we are all different. Somewhere in all of us is an addiction screaming to get out and control. At times we hide our difference. Some people die never having been known. How can this be easy?

Once you begin to face your difference and accept it deep within yourself, it becomes harder and more painful to live a lie. The price of forever pleasing people gets to be too much. Think how much effort, heartache and pain goes into pleasing all those people 24 hours a day. I remember feeling guilty if the postman did not smile. A car honks his horn in the next street and we say,

"Sorry." Every telephone call is an expected emergency or termination from the office.

It is crazy. It is sick. It is the disease. It is okay for me to say, "No." I do not need permission to live. The lie of the century is "I'm fine."

Some weeks ago, I heard about a lady who was knocked off her bicycle by a car. It was the driver's fault for not stopping. She apologized and tried to cycle home.

A man confided in me that he felt guilty and awkward making an emergency call to the Fire Department when his garage caught fire.

Think of the suicides. Imagine the guilt feelings expressed in the farewell notes. "I do not wish to be a burden any longer, and so . . ."

"Nobody understands how lonely and different I feel. Therefore, I have . . ."

"I cannot please . . ."

It is so refreshing to meet an individualist, a person willing to say "no" or "I don't want to do that." A priest I know was asked by a parishioner on leaving church, "Will you pray for me, Father?" The priest replied, "Surely. But have you thought about praying yourself?"

Part of the attraction of the man Gandhi was that he believed in and respected his own individuality. He could live with difference. He owned his difference. He could not accept or understand intolerance and bigotry. He represented to the world God's gift of freedom to mankind. Any form of slavery was abhorrent to him. Nobody can imprison, beat or kill the spirit of man. He is forever free. Gandhi taught his people to walk on water. His Spirituality and tolerance is captured in his statement, "An eye for an eye makes the whole world blind."

The soul of a man lives within his difference,
his uniqueness,
his specialness.

His Spirituality is in his difference. You cannot arrest, chain, hurt or kill my difference, because it does not belong to you.

It comes from God.

In Him I am different and unique.

All we need do is accept the gift.

To deny it or run away from it, is to be unworthy of His gift.

It is you.

Let us take an aspect of difference that many deny and run away from. Gayness. In no way do I consider gayness a disease or a sickness. I am using it simply as an example of difference. Thousands of people are in denial of their gayness. They refuse to face, accept, own their true selves, their true sexuality, their true feelings. They grow up different, and live the lie of hiding their difference. It leads to hypocrisy, prejudice and pain.

The suppression and fear of homosexuality can lead to the disease of homophobia. Homophobia is negative and destructive and can suffocate the God-given Spirituality in man. It stops you from loving, caring and understanding gay people. It is a kind of sexual anti-semitism. Gays are seen as the lowest form of life.

The scum of the earth.

A plague on mankind.

To be exterminated.

Homophobia is like any other form of obsession and compulsion in that it feeds on lies, anger, loneliness, manipulation and pain. Ego trips and feelings of superiority abound. The main symptom is denial.

It afflicts those who beat up gays.

It afflicts those who are forever criticizing and speaking against gays.

It afflicts those wanting to know who is gay in the workplace.

These people, if asked, would maintain that they are revealing a normal interest in a serious problem!

The disease of homophobia is fed by hate and prejudice. The long-term goals are divisive and destructive. Homophobia often masks a feeling of inferiority and loneliness, reflecting personal pain and self-hatred. As with the disease of addiction, the dynamics need to be understood. The homophobic needs to be loved and understood, and gently led to self-acceptance and integration.

Many males afflicted with homophobia pretend to be "real" men. They build up muscles, swagger around the streets, look theatrically strong and tough, act "macho", and dress accordingly.

Another form of homophobia involves the W.A.S.P. (White Anglo-Saxon Protestant) look. Neat, clean and ever-so-plain. Ties and office shirts are mandatory, even on vacation. Grey is their favorite color. Red is avoided like poison. A tense, controlled outlook on life is revealed, even when you ask to borrow the garden spade. Incidentally, the garage, garden and workroom are always in order. To be caught with a dirty car would be like dropping your pants in public; embarrassing, humiliating and human.

Many homophobics discover a "high" and "buzz" in hating.

Hating gays and Communists. The two are often irrationally connected. Homophobics avoid looking too deeply at themselves. Like all drug users, they manipulate the hate and prejudice to escape. They are in pain, but too proud to ask for help. The pain is the basis of their disease.

The homophobic at times feels his pain. He gets in touch with his loneliness, fear and isolation. The gay boogeyman in his life has too much power, power that his homophobia is giving it. The boogeyman reflects something of himself. In the hate and violence is something of himself. He is hating himself. His excessive denial suggests guilt. So long as the homophobic refuses to get honest, continues to hide his real self, denies any personal involvement with his feelings, he will remain lost and alone. The gay boogeyman's energy and strength come from the buried fear of homophobia. Once you confront the boogeyman, talk about the boogeyman, uncover the hiding place of the boogeyman, you discover yourself. Discover that little bit of difference you have been hiding. Discover that little bit of difference that makes us human. That is walking on water.

Those writers involved in the study of human sexuality often prefer the word "gayness" to homosexuality because it means more than sexual activity. Gayness is saying more about a person than what he/she does in bed. Gayness involves bringing your homosexual feelings into a concern about politics, the world, art and literature, about life and loving. Gayness has that spiritual dimension that adds soul to the loving and living. Gayness is involved in the encouraging eye, the gentle touch and the soft spoken word. Gayness is a wholistic approach to the homosexual's life.

If you are a homophobic and in denial of your gayness, then you need to recognize it. Recognize it and come to accept it. Know it. The life you are living with your friends and family is a pretense. A sham. Gay feelings do not go away with time. Being gay is like having white skin and green eyes, it is who you are. You could pretend to date girls and please your family. Get married and have children. Work away your life at being what you are not. But it is a lie. It is a sad, tragic, and painful lie. It is the ultimate sickness in pleasing people, and all the time you know. You grow old being a fake. No wonder if in the progression of your disease you get resentful and angry.

At times you will want to fight the whole world. Other times you will just fight the happy and relaxed gays. Always you will be fighting yourself.

On numerous occasions you will catch a glimpse of who you really are. What you really feel.

Driving down the street, you see the walking bodies and you think.

Lying on the beach, you look and think.

With the TV drama, you look and think.

Always, your feelings, buried deep within, tell you. They are real.

Homophobia, an aspect of the disease, is part of the Great Lie.

So you are different? So what? Your sexuality is a statement of who you are. The variety of God's creation will always baffle and confuse little men. Big men will learn to grow with it. With the moment of recognition and acceptance come the choices.

Are you to live in the shadows or the light? Both can be painful. Open and free. Cloistered and imprisoned.

Your sexuality can be creative and loving or corrupt and diseased. Gay or heterosexual, the temptations are the same. Reality or fantasy. Which? Sexuality can be listening and gentle or aggressive and using. The choice is yours. Make no mistake, the wrong choice is a decision for the disease, for the compulsion, for the obsession. Then we will meet the age-old symptoms: anger, resentment, isolation, loneliness, fear and cruel indifference. It is a sexual dry-drunk. Dull, boring and overrated.

There is another way to grow. The open softness that reveals the vulnerability of love. The joyous and enthusiastic sharing of that which is different. The revealed courage and strength of risk. The creative shared truthfulness that enables the privileged listener to locate his own forgotten difference.

In the acknowledged memory is the one-ness. Such a sharing becomes another insight into the given Spirituality.

To listen and to hear is Godly recognition.

Serenity says, "Your feelings, although different, are my feelings. They are the same. I have felt like that. I hope I will feel that way again."

In the difference is the many. In the many is the One. Gay relationships, like heterosexual relationships, will continue to grow in the atmosphere of honest and creative acceptance. What started as difference becomes variety. That is Spirituality.

William Blake says, "What matters is that we should move. Be always moving. That is what counts, this, and how we move."

I am not afraid of my difference anymore. It is not a barrier, but a bridge to Divine Understanding. My being an alcoholic, having a disease, being a minority, unites me with millions. The symptoms only appear different. The disease is the same.

More than this, I am discovering that only my outsides look different from yours. My insides, my God-given Spirituality, that is the same. When I read about the death of the Elephant Man, read his words, I cry, I smile, I think and then I get excited. I feel his difference. It is in me.

> *Some six months after Merrick's return from the country, he was found dead in bed. This was April, 1890. He was lying on his back as if asleep, and had evidently died suddenly and without a struggle, since not even the coverlet of the bed was disturbed. The method of his death was peculiar. So large and so heavy was his head that he could not sleep lying down. When he assumed the recumbent position, the massive skull was inclined to drop backwards, with the result that he experienced no little distress. The attitude he was compelled to assume when he slept was very strange. He sat up in bed with his back supported by pillows, his knees were drawn up, and his arms clasped round his legs, while his head rested on the points of his bent knees.*
>
> *He often said to me that he wished he could lie down to sleep "like other people". I think on this last night, he must, with some determination, have made the experiment. The pillow was soft, and the head when placed on it, must have fallen backwards and caused a dislocation of the neck. Thus it came about that his death was due to the desire that had dominated his life—the pathetic, but hopeless desire to be "like other people".[1]*

The tragedy is that John Merrick could not accept his difference. He died trying to be the same. Although he had been courageous with his disease, noble in his attitudes, loving and vulnerble in his lifestyle, still that small part of his obsession and compulsion got him in the end. That part of him that was his difference, that inability to sleep like others, he would not own. It made him attempt the unreal. It made him live for a moment the fantasy. John died trying to be like you and me. His final act of desperate people-pleasing killed him.

As Shakespeare said, "We know what we are, but not what we may be."

[1]*The True History of the Elephant Man,* Michael Howell and Peter Form.

8 MEDITATION

The way to walk on water is to understand yourself. The key to living is an awareness of yourself; the miracle is within. Meditation is an aid to walking on water and in this chapter I hope to give some easy techniques for meditation.

Addiction is escape. It is choosing "fantasy" instead of "reality". Wanting to be somebody else, pretending to be happy when you are sad, appearing in control when you are falling apart inside. A man drinks to avoid problems; a student uses marijuana to please his friends and be "hip"; a young girl eats behind her anger and boredom. Drugs supposedly take the pain out of life, but in reality they progressively erode away the meaning of life. Addiction is loneliness, isolation and a constant feeling of being "less than". The addict is saying to life, "I'm out for lunch!"

Unfortunately, meditation is seen by some to be an escape from life, a trip into ecstacy, a journey from the material world into a transcendental bliss; a kind of spiritual high. Christian mystics and Eastern gurus have sometimes presented the view that

our bodies,

the world,

this life is sick and corrupt.

We need to escape from the prison of the physical body by the use of meditation. Thousands of people over the years have disappeared into the deserts and mountains or entered temples and ashrams in order to find a "peace" that they believed could not be experienced in ordinary living. They closed the door on their old life, they left behind family and friends and they sought a meaning elsewhere.

Not everybody, thank God, sees meditation in this exclusive way, but still the man in the street fears and avoids meditation because of where it might lead. To use an English expression, "Meditation is decidedly foreign. Not to be done in polite society. Rather like sex, it tends to scare the horses!"

In my opinion, the truth is the opposite: It does not scare the horses and it should not scare us. Meditation is a technique of realizing our full potential as human beings and living our lives to the fullest. It is about finding the time and discovering the energy "to be." It is placing the physical, mental and emotional aspects of our lives in an "at-one-ment."

It is using silence to say "yes."

Meditation is part of the God-given gift of Spirituality.

It is feeling who we are and giving it to the world.

It is exploring the reality of the present.

Meditation has much to say to the alcoholic, drug addict, and overeater, but it is also an art in life that would benefit everybody.

With meditation comes acceptance,

> growth,

>> serenity.

It is not just for religious people: priests, rabbis, mullahs, monks, nuns and gurus, or eccentrics in the desert. Meditation is for shy Alice in the grocery shop; Johnny, who is angry at the world because his parents are alcoholic; Ann, who is recovering from anorexia; Jack, who is facing a cancer operation; young Harry, a drug addict, who is contemplating suicide. Meditation is for Bill and Carol who were just married and planning a family; George and Phillip, who celebrate a ten-year relationship; Harry, a widower, who gratefully remembers his married years. Meditation fits life.

It helps form answers to those begging questions that all human beings must face:

> Who am I?
> What am I?
> Where am I going?

We think too small. We exclude joy from our world because we think and feel most things are not for us. We also foolishly segregate life into compartments, pigeonholes, divisions—and we remain impoverished.

We decided meditation was for

saints,
clever people,
foreigners,
fanatics,
non-Christians,
eccentrics.

It is for these—and more!

We decided that to meditate you must—

wear funny clothes,
say Hindu words,
kneel for hours,
put incense in your room,
fast on bread and water,
avoid sex,
use mantras,
experience a trance.

It involves these—and more!

Truth is always in the "more."

You do not need to study "spiritual" books, pass religious tests, or have a pronounced hankering for God in order to meditate. You need only a desire. Meditation allows you to experience God and life. It allows you to experience you. All of you. Divinity in our grasp.

Meditation brings relaxation,

compatibility,
energy,
light,
peace.

Enough.

What is it?

Webster's Dictionary defines meditation as "deep reflection on sacred matters as a devotional act." However, meditation is not so much about doing, getting, or achieving something, as it is about being,

experiencing,
realizing,
discovering ourselves.

Meditation relives the tremendous truth depicted on the Sistine Chapel ceiling in Rome by Michaelangelo, where God is touching the fingertip of Adam—at that point the spark of the Divine is given! In the created is the Creator, the miracle of being man.

So in the discovery of ourselves, we will ultimately find God.

"Be still and know that I am God."[1]

In the context of this book, meditation is:

> being in touch with our feelings,
>> being in a relationship with oneself,
>>> being whole.

Be Still and Know that I Am God

It is holding you in the stillness of your life.
As the Psalmist says, "Be still—and know that I am God.
　　　　"Be still—and know
　　　　"Be still—
　　　　"Be . . ."
Explore the stillness that lives in you. Remember, meditation is not difficult. The hardest part of meditation is deciding to do it!

Meditation is a technique. There are certain actions or procedures that should be taken to aid relaxation, awareness, stillness. The obvious needs to be said, proper rest and diet is necessary. I do not intend to legislate about hours of sleep or what foods should be avoided, but balance, rest and nutrition are an important prerequisite for any meditation exercise— essential for the recovering addict. Many good health books are available, and add that important ingredient to self-awareness, "at-one-ment" and the creative art of self-love.

How long should you meditate? When you are beginning, a few minutes will be enough.

Remember, most of us tend to be obsessive and compulsive about achievement and success. This will sabotage our meditation technique. In the first few months, ten minutes or less will be sufficient. After experiencing meditation, the length of time will vary, but the qualitative consistency will remain constant. Your body will begin to tell you what you need.

A.　**The "Be Still" Technique**
　　Go to a place where you can be alone.
　　Make yourself comfortable.
　　Be still.

　　To get to the feeling of inner peace, we must first listen to the world.
　　Hear the noises that surround your life—
　　　　　　　　　　cars,
　　　　　　　　　　　birds,
　　　　　　　　　　　　rain,
　　　　　　　　　　　　　　people shouting in the streets.
　　After listening to these noises for a few moments, leave them outside
　　and listen to the noises within your room.
　　　Concentrate on the clock ticking,
　　　　　　　　　　fridge buzzing,
　　　　　　　　　　　fire crackling,
　　　　　　　　　　　　dog sighing.
　　Then come from the noises in your room to yourself.

Spend a few moments enjoying and exploring yourself.
Touch your legs,
   thighs,
      stomach,
         arms,
            neck,
               face.
You are important. Remind yourself you are unique,
                        special,
                              divine.
The breath of God was first breathed into Adam, now it breathes in you.
   Hear yourself breathing.
   Feel yourself breathing.
      Relax in your breathing.
         Enjoy you.
            Be still.

B. **Gratitude Technique**
   Do the "be still" technique, and then:
   Focus on a part of your body or an aspect of creation that you enjoy.
   Either look at it, touch it, or imagine it.
   Be grateful.
   Suggestions:
      The eye,
         A tree,
            A friend,
               My hand,
                  A stream.

C. **Word Technique**
   Do the "be still" technique, then:
   Bring into your mind "a word", a word that you value.
   For a few moments, explore that word, bringing its energy into your life.
   Suggestions:
      Joy,
         Peace,
            Love,
               Serenity.
   Needless to say, the use of a "mantra", a chosen word or sound that means something to you, and only you, can be used with this technique. Although the use of a "mantra" is Hindu, it has been found to be useful for people with other religious backgrounds —

or none. Anything that makes sense to you and is positive and creative can be used. Do not be "narrow" in your thinking.

D.   **Breathing Technique**
Do the "be still" technique, then:
Concentrate on breathing "in" and "out".
Feel your body breathing, experience the breathing, slowly mouth a word that fits your rhythm.
Breathe that word into your being.
Let that energy breathe through your being.
Example:
  So-ber
   So-ber
    So-ber.
Suggestions:
  Hon-esty
   Seren-ity
    Je-sus
     Ho-ly

Remember, meditation is an experience: the experience is you. Nothing should be manufactured or fake. Meditation is real and it has been given. You possess it all. It is but a part of the miracle of being you.

This is Spirituality.

This is walking on water.

With the aid of meditation, I can feel alive without the need to drink alcohol, smoke a joint, or use a drug. And everything that I experience is real. Meditation enables me to live with all the various aspects of my life.

When I am tense,
anxious,
lonely,
afraid.
When I am creating,
writing articles,
preparing sermons,
lecturing to patients.
When I am playing,
walking along the beach,
enjoying friendships,
being physical.

Meditation awakens that spark of the Divine that exists within me and holds it in my life.

Meditation reminds me—my space is my home.

The Serenity Prayer

God grant me the
Serenity to accept the things
I cannot change:

Courage to change the things
*   I can; and*
Wisdom to know the difference.

Living one day at a time;
Enjoying one moment at a time;
Accepting hardship
As the pathway to peace;

Taking, as He did, this sinful
*   world as it is, not as I would*
*   have it;*

Trusting that He will make all
*   things right, if I surrender*
*   to His Will;*

That I may be reasonably happy
*   in this life, and supremely*
*   happy with Him forever in*
*   the next. Amen.*

Reinhold Niebuhr

[1]Psalms 46:11.

9 RELATIONSHIPS

The spiritual life teaches us that we are powerful human beings. We make the difference in the living of our lives. We are capable of creating a healthier life,
>   healthier relationships,
>   a healthier world.

We are not just automated robots but spiritual creatures who have the power to determine our destiny. In the living of our lives we create success or failure. Nothing just happens. Things happen as a direct result of the decisions, actions and beliefs we manifest in our lives. This is an important awareness and it can make all the difference to our recovery — and continued recovery — as human beings.

In the earlier chapter entitled "Spirituality", I told the story of the two little fish that were afraid to swim out into the ocean. They huddled together in fear and missed life. We can do this in relationships. The fear of being rejected, the fear of not being good enough or the fear of not being able to sustain a relationship keeps us victims of loneliness and isolation. **Often we seem to prefer the security of loneliness to the risked possibility of happiness.** When we first hear this sentence, it sounds crazy. How could anyone prefer painful isolation to the creative possibility of a loving relationship? But fear creates atrophy.

We become immobile.

We isolate.

We must place this understanding of fear in the context of an increasingly addictive society. Fear is a symptom of addiction. It is a symptom of co-dependency. It is a symptom of those millions of children who grew up in a dysfunctional home. In the chaos of addiction, with its associated reverberations throughout family, church and society, many are affected. Few people are spared. We live in an addicted society. We live in an obsessive and compulsive world.

Just consider some of the addictions, some of the compulsive behaviors that exist: alcoholism; drug addiction; gambling; men and women who love too much; compulsive overeating with its related disorders of diets, use of diuretics or laxatives, self-induced vomiting; religious addiction; sexual addiction; compulsive spending; obsessive physical exercise; workaholism, prescription drug abuse; compulsive television viewing; co-dependency symptoms and other abuse issues related to all of the above. Then add the millions of children who become dysfunctional as a result of growing up in these addicted and abusive homes. Is anyone spared?

If you have to take a drug, look a certain shape, have somebody in order to be somebody, then the fear of not being good enough, having enough or looking good enough will affect the living of your life. And the spiritual power of self-acceptance is lost.

Relationships obviously are affected. The major areas of relationships are:

a) Ourselves
b) Other people
c) God

Although I have placed God last in the order of significant relationships, it does not mean that I consider our relationship with God the least important. On the contrary; I consider our relationship with God (as we understand Him or Her) to be essential, pervasive and the key to the discovery of the spiritual life. However, it is also my belief that God is manifested in this world, in creation, in people. If we do not develop a relationship with ourselves, if we do not embark on the journey into self, then I do not believe we can comprehend the reality of God in the universe. In order to understand God, *we need to understand.*

God has chosen to work through people: prophets, seers, writers, priests, musicians, artists, scientists, psychologists, lovers and friends. Because God is truly involved in His creation, He reveals Himself, proclaims Himself, makes miracle through the exercise of human relationships and communication. In our relationships with other people, we hear the promises of God. Therefore, when we have developed a healthy relationship with ourselves and other people, we are ready to apprehend, meaningfully, our relationship with God.

Without relationships we cannot live effectively. We may exist, painfully, but we will never experience the abundance of the spiritual life. Only when we feel good about ourselves, good about ourselves in relationship to others, will we be able to understand what it means to be a child of God. The energizing joy of self-love creates healthy relationships with others. Therefore, in our pursuit of the spiritual life, we need to consider relationships.

Healthy relationships are essential for the living of the spiritual life. You cannot live life in isolation; the impetus for creative living exists within ourselves. As we have said earlier in this book, the miracle is within. We are the miracle. We are the center of our universe. Everything that is created emanates from within.

The God as we understand Him or Her is dependent on our willingness and determination to discover God in our world.

Our relationship with lovers, family, friends and associates is dependent on the attitudes and behavioral styles we adopt.

Our influence on the neighborhood, job market and country is dependent on the apprehension of our spiritual power.

Relationships emanate from self!

The spiritual life creates healthy relationships. Loving relation-ships do not just happen. There is an art to love. As with so many aspects of living, we need to develop an expertise in achieving precision, confidence and consistency. Nobody just starts out playing the piano. We must practice, learn the language of music, comprehend what we are doing wrong and develop skills to improve style and performance. The joy of being a pianist is the result of work and effort.

No one just sits down and starts writing poetry for the first time. The poet needs to develop his craft. He needs to finely tune his feelings for words, sentence construction and the form in which he is to write. The poet must spend time with the tools of his artistry, selecting carefully those words that have inner resonance to convey his message. Poetry is an art that requires effort.

The art of developing a relationship is much the same. Relationships are more than acquaintanceships. They involve the desire to know and be known. They require a willingness to understand and be understood. Relationships take time to develop and there is a learning process involved in each relationship. Naturally there will be mistakes. Because human beings are not perfect, our relationships will not be perfect. Yet our desire to develop the spiritual life requires that we seek a personal improvement that leads to health and recovery. Remember, we desire to be the best human beings that we can be, developing the best loving relationships that we can achieve.

How do we develop a guide to healthy, loving and meaningful relationships? It is a common maxim that we can learn from our mistakes. Acknowledged mistakes can become the focal point for improvement. In the dynamic concept of surrender, admitting our faults and accepting our involvement in our dysfunctional behavior, we begin the process of recovery: spiritual recovery. Therefore, when we become honestly aware of the problems in our relationship, a moment of healing is grasped. Confronting the dysfunction is the key to developing healthier and loving relationships.

For those who work a Twelve-Step program, this concept might offer a creative insight into the phrase, "Turn it over". The emphasis is on making the decision to turn our lives in a new direction. The responsibility for turning it over rests in our decision, willingness or desire to risk facing a different direction in life. But before we can turn ourselves in a different direction, we need to know — really know — which way we are facing.

We must understand down before we can know up.

We must understand west before we can know east.

We need to know in before we can go out.

We need to know sick before we can get well.

Let me emphasize that last statement:

We need to know sick before we can get well.

Healthy relationships are dependent on our determination to recognize and confront what constitutes sick relationships. Let us look at some of the characteristics that create unhealthy relationships:

1. Closed, narrow, bigoted, controlling —

   A relationship cannot develop and grow if it excludes the possibility of change. So many relationships die because they create the atmosphere of a prison; life becomes a chained existence rather than an experience of unlimited possibilities. The fear of confronting the new and unfamiliar makes some people want to "control" the adventure of a relationship. The fear of people, places and things that are different produces a prejudiced and bigoted outlook on life.

2. Silent, moody, selfish, resentful —

It is emotionally painful to live with someone you do not know and who does not want to be known. People can use silence as a weapon to abuse their partners; it becomes a passive form of violence. A cruel selfishness is involved in this silent torture. An unwillingness to share not only reveals buried resentments but creates resentments in others.

3. Aggressive, violent, angry, jealous —

The root of so much aggression and violence is fear. The fear may be the result of childhood issues or drug-related characteristics. However, the need to dominate the relationship through violence often is the motivating factor. Here we have an example of fear creating fear that eventually destroys the possibility of a relationship.

4. Low self-esteem, lies, manipulation, people-pleasing —

You cannot please all the people all of the time. If one or both partners in a relationship are so lacking in positive self-worth, then they might create the illusion of success and happiness with lies and manipulation. The relationship becomes another facet of this dysfunctional illusion. Honesty is the basis of any healthy relationship.

5. Rigid, uncompromising, proud, arrogant —

Any relationship requires a willingness to bend. We are not God and to refuse to compromise in life is to destroy any possibility of dialogue. The tragedy is that the proud person usually is in emotional pain but refuses to express his need of others. Such rigidity bleeds feelings from any relationship.

6. Selfish, egotistical, thoughtless, spoiled —

Many children who are spoiled by their parents, given everything they ever wanted at their slightest whim, grow up to be dysfunctionally selfish. They become lost and hurt in a world that refuses to respond to their wants and needs like their doting parents. Such people are unable to create a relationship because they are thoughtless. Their obsessive infatuation with their needs eventually destroys them.

7. Emotionally cold, unaffectionate, detached, unresponsive —
Many adults who were hurt in their childhood, having been emotionally and sexually abused, often are unable to create a physical contact in relationships. The past abuse haunts them into adulthood, making them prisoners of an unresponsiveness that keeps other people locked out.

8. Isolated, uncommunicative, lonely, boring —
All relationships are based on people wanting to come together — to know and be known. To isolate or restrict communication eventually destroys a relationship. Self-induced isolation also creates a boring loneliness that keeps people away because there is nothing adventuresome, exciting or attractive about isolation.

9. Health problems (hungry, angry, lonely, tired) —
A healthy person has the possibility of being an exciting person. To neglect health through poor diet, repression of feelings, self-induced isolation and an abuse of work or sleep is an escape from reality; it also is spiritually irresponsible. God does not make junk. Our physical, emotional and mental well-being is our responsibility as creative creatures; to neglect important health issues is to hinder the possibility of healthy relationships.

10. Negative, destructive, cynical, pessimistic —
Any healthy relationship is a positive statement about life. To develop and sustain negative and pessimistic attitudes and behavior patterns is to destroy the creative momentum of a relationship. Relationships are part of our spiritual "yes to life".

In my daily meditation book, *Say Yes To Life,* I wrote this about relationships:

> *Spirituality is about being willing to reach out into new areas, engage in new and different relationships, enjoy the richness of God's world. As I grow in sobriety, I develop the capacity to react differently to painful situations and overcome them. I learn that mistakes can make for new conquests. That lasting joys and achievements are born in the risk.*

We now have clearly seen the characteristics that create and sustain dysfunctional relationships. All the above characteristics would destroy any relationship with:

a) Ourselves
b) Other people
c) God

How can we claim to love God if by our attitude and behavior we are destroying any meaningful relationship with other people? How can we grow and develop spiritually as human beings if we have isolated ourselves from any creative relationship with others? God is primarily apprehended and discovered in our relationship with ourselves and other people.

In confronting the characteristics of a dysfunctional relationship, we are able to identify the goals for developing and sustaining healthy relationships. We can only "turn it over" when we see what it is that needs to be changed. In confronting the dysfunction, we are brought into the joy of a spiritual recovery.

Suggestions for a healthy relationship with ourselves, other people and God include:

1. Accept criticism gratefully, being appreciative of the opportunity to improve.
2. Do not indulge in self-pity.
3. Do not expect special consideration from anyone.
4. Seek to express your feelings responsibly.
5. Realize that no person or situation is wholly good or bad.
6. Seek to endure defeat and disappointment without whining or complaining.
7. Do not worry unduly about things that are not your responsibility.
8. Do not boast or "show off" in socially unacceptable ways.
9. Enjoy the success and good fortune of others.
10. Remain open-minded and listen thoughtfully to the opinions of others.
11. Do not harbor resentments.
12. Remember that nobody is perfect; we are not God.

RELAPSE

Relapse is a progressive behavior pattern that, if not confronted, talked about and seriously dealt with, will lead to an active dysfunctional lifestyle — either a return to alcoholic drinking, use of mind-altering chemicals, destructive eating patterns, sexual acting-out, workaholism, compulsive gambling, co-dependent behavior or the myriad of painful feelings that adult children have sought to recover from. In a sentence, relapse results in addictive or destructive behavior.

Spirituality is the antidote for relapse because the power of knowing that we are creative children of God (the God as we understand Him or Her) becomes the positive factor that enables recovery. Spirituality is knowing, on a daily basis, that we are positive and creative human beings and that we have the capacity, which already has been given by God in creation, to arrest dysfunctional behavior.

We are the miracle.

We make the difference.

In the living of our lives God is activated.

A pioneer book on relapse prevention is *Staying Sober* by Terence T. Gorski and Merlene Miller. This book states:

*Recovery from addiction is like walking up a down
escalator. It is impossible to stand still. When you stop moving
forward, you find yourself moving backwards. You do not
have to do anything in particular to develop symptoms that
lead to relapse. All you need to do is to fail to take recovery
steps. The symptoms develop spontaneously in the absence of
a strong recovery program. Once you abandon a recovery
program, it is only a matter of time until the symptoms of
past acute withdrawal appear, and if nothing is done to
manage them, you will experience a period of out-of-control
behavior that we call the relapse syndrome. Loss of control of
past acute withdrawal symptoms results in the relapse
syndrome.*[1]

The emphasis that is made in the book on developing a strong
and comprehensive recovery program is also a plea for spirituality:
Spirituality is recovery. The awareness that we make the difference
in our lives — that things begin to happen when we activate them
in our daily decisions, that wellness is directly related to attitudinal
and behavioral changes we are prepared to make — this
awareness constitutes a spiritual awakening.

What does the concept of "relapse" mean as it relates to
chemical addiction and compulsive behavior? It does not simply
mean returning to alcoholic drinking or mind-altering drug use.
Just as we have begun to understand that sobriety is more than
"not drinking", so relapse is a progressive behavior pattern that
leads to a negative and destructive lifestyle — and the person may
not have returned to active drug use. It is certainly true that many
people who are caught in the relapse syndrome do return to
chemical usage, but it is important to remember that people can
be in a state of relapse for many years and not be using any mind-
altering drug; indeed, they may never use. However, and this
cannot be stressed enough, they are not experiencing the joy,
freedom and creativity of sobriety.

The relapse syndrome does not just apply to alcoholism and
drug users. The relapse process is applicable to all dysfunctional
lifestyles that have previously sought a recovery program. Those at
risk will include: alcoholics, drug users, bulimics, prescription
drug users, sex addicts, workaholics, religious addicts, men and
women who love too much, nicotine addicts, compulsive
gamblers, co-dependents to all these compulsive behaviors, plus

the millions of adult children who grew up in these dysfunctional homes. It is not too extravagant to suggest that the country — the nation — is often at various stages of relapse. Government agencies, school boards, industry and the church all can share the relapse symptoms of denial that make them minimize the seriousness or damage that addiction is causing our society. We all are at risk.

Relapse is when we miss for an hour, a day, a week or a year that creative potential we have as human beings; we miss the spiritual promise of wellness. To avoid Truth is to choose The Lie. To give in to the relapse syndrome is to become children of The Lie.

Because relapse is an addictive process, it has symptoms, characteristics or signs that reveal its presence. Our spiritual recovery rests in recognizing and confronting these symptoms.

Those in relapse will begin to exhibit the behavior patterns and attitudes that they practiced when they were using drugs or were dysfunctional. The relapse person is taking steps *backward* toward a powerless and unmanageable lifestyle.

These high risk characteristics include:

A. **Negative attitudes and behaviors**

1. Inappropriate expressions of anger, violence, sarcasm, rudeness, selfishness and thoughtlessness
2. Unwillingness to resolve guilt and shame issues
3. Extreme feelings of helplessness and hopelessness
4. Unrealistic fears and anxieties
5. Extreme nervousness and tension in non-threatening situations
6. Boredom with recovery program and life in general
7. No creative or satisfying leisure interests
8. A denial or minimizing of past problems
9. A recognizable and continuing depression
10. A development of cross-addictive behavior patterns, such as gambling, sex, food, work, relationships and exercise
11. Exhibiting long periods of exhaustion, fatigue and apathy
12. Impatient with recovery program and life; nothing happening quickly enough
13. Progressive isolation from recovery people
14. Arrogant statements concerning recovery program, e.g., "I'll never drink, use or behave that way again."
15. A preoccupation with past dysfunctional behavior

16. Unwilling to express or deal with resentments
17. Long bouts of self-pity

B. **Problems in relationships that relate to relapse**
    1. Argumentative with others
    2. Difficulty experienced in meeting new friends and developing relationships
    3. Unwillingness to trust others
    4. Isolation from recovering friends
    5. Friendships developed with people who use and have dysfunctional behavior patterns
    6. Sexual problems such as fear of sex, impotence, lack of control concerning sexual feelings, inappropriate sexual behavior
    7. Inability to handle responsibilities with family or friends

C. **High pressure situations**
    1. Success in employment or coping with unemployment
    2. Difficulty handling evenings or weekends
    3. Overwhelmed by the ordinary stresses and anxieties of life
    4. Lack of objectives or goals in life
    5. Inability to cope with physical pain or problems
    6. Desire to be surrounded by alcohol or past dysfunctional behavior at holidays or birthdays

Spiritual Recovery Program

The key to recovery from relapse is to recognize these symptoms and other behavior patterns that are reminiscent of past dysfunctional behavior and to confront them, talk about them and deal with them. Some people might need to go back into treatment for their relapse issues. Others should contact a relapse therapist. But for many it will mean returning to that Twelve-Step program that created relief from their addictive and compulsive behaviors years or months past. Perhaps for those who refused to get involved in a Twelve-Step program, the time for surrender to a different way of coping with their addictive nature has arrived. The fellowship that has been created around the Twelve-Step program throughout the world is based on action, not talk; it is about making decisions that lead to change; and the spiritual awakening comes in knowing, in God's love, we can achieve recovery.

For any person who recognizes (in their attitudes and behavior) some of the relapse symptoms that have been discussed above, the time to act is now; procrastination is not only dangerous but is a symptom of relapse. The person in relapse, regardless of years of so-called sobriety or how many conferences he has attended or spoken at, needs to return humbly and joyfully to the first five steps of the Twelve-Step program. No one has ever said that you cannot retrace your steps. Recovery is a process, not an event. It is a circle, not a straight line. We can return to the beginnings of our spiritual recovery.

1. We admitted that we were powerless over alcohol — that our lives had become unmanageable.
2. Come to believe that a Power greater than ourselves could restore us to sanity.
3. Made a decision to turn our will and our lives over to the care of God, as we understood Him.
4. Made a searching and fearless moral inventory of ourselves.
5. Admitted to God, to ourselves and to another human being the exact nature of our wrongs.

You might say this is easier said than done. But is it easier to go back to the pain, powerlessness and unmanageability of past behavior? I believe it is easier to get healthy and stay healthy than it is to remain dysfunctional or return to addictive behavior. Why? Because all compulsive and obsessive behavior is destructive, destroying every area of life and personal happiness. The reason that people relapse is that they choose to forget their past pain, minimizing the agonizing consequences of their addiction, denying the past losses in their lives.

Elie Weiss, the famous Jewish poet and philosopher, was asked the question, "Why do you keep talking and writing about the Holocaust?"

His reply was pertinent to this discussion: "If people are not reminded, if people choose to forget the tragedy of the Holocaust and its effects on and for humanity, then it will all come back."

This is also true for relapse. The relapse syndrome is a series of progressive choices to escape the reality of our true selves, our true natures, who we really are; relapse is a cunning and powerful aspect of denial.

Spirituality is about reality. It is about taking responsibility as creative creatures for the quality of our lives, the quality of our relationships and the quality of our world. Spirituality confronts and stops our dance into death. It makes us ask the three basic questions of life and come up with answers that relate to our ongoing recovery as human beings.

    1. Who are we?
    2. What are we?
    3. Where are we going?

I answered these questions many years ago when I was new in recovery and I have consistently sought to remind myself of the echoing answers I once gave:

    1. I am a child of God.
    2. I am a recovering alcoholic.
    3. I am returning to my spiritual home.

A long time ago I learned that no one can fix Leo.

The spiritual program is always personal, basing itself on a God as I understand Him or Her. The qualities I attribute to God I should seek to reveal in my life. The God that I believe in needs to be manifested in my actions and attitudes. Anything less would be hypocrisy.

If I believe in a God of Truth, then I should be truthful.

If I believe in a God of Acceptance, then I should accept others.

If I believe in a God of Forgiveness, then I should forgive.

If I believe in a God of Change, then I should be prepared to change.

In my life my God is revealed.

[1]Terence T. Gorski and Merlene Miller, *Staying Sober,* p. 29.

11 | TREATMENT

Spirituality is our "yes to life". It is knowing that God loves us so much that He or She is involved in our lives. It is understanding that whatever the problems might be, we have the capacity within ourselves to seek and find the solution. Spirituality is recognizing divinity in the choices that we make, the decisions we implement in our lives.

Alan Ecclestone explains it this way:

> The Yes to God means something more. There is the right response that all creation could be said to yearn to make, the creaturely desire, however buried and distorted it may be at times, to be itself, to be the work of God, which with a fine audacity the writer of Genesis will describe as being 'very good'. Right faith in God expects it to be so expressed. "Sing, O ye heavens; for the Lord hath done it: Shout, ye lower parts of the earth; break forth into singing, ye mountains, O forest and every tree therein; for the Lord hath redeemed Jacob, and glorified himself in Israel."
>
> This is the Yes that every man and woman, inside and outside churches, inside other faiths or none at all, will be striving to be human, express in some degree in unremembered acts or in self-giving with a dedicated life. Its roots are in compassion, appreciation, delight, tenderness and love. Its

growth is manifest in works of mercy, healing, education, justice, social welfare, respect for things and creatures of every kind. Its flowering is in art and science, in marriage, parental love and all commitment to delighted patient use of human powers.

For many years people have talked about the program of recovery as being spiritual, emphasizing that there is not a spiritual aspect to the program but the "whole" program is spiritual. If this is true for recovery, it must also be true in treatment, because it is (hopefully) in treatment that recovery begins.

Earlier in this book, I sought to make the important distinction between spirituality and religion, between denominationalism and the all-inclusive power of spirituality. Many people have been helped to understand the difference by this important but succinct saying: "Religion is man-made; Spirituality is God-given."

The essential contribution that Spirituality makes in the treatment process concerns God's indiscriminate Love; nobody is excluded. God really does love all his children equally, in spite of our imperfections. We no longer need to look at life from the outside; we are created to be involved. Our membership into living started at our creation.

This is a very important message for all addicts, co-dependents and adult children to hear; regardless of race, culture, sexual orientation or dysfunction, we are loved by God. Now we need to begin to love ourselves. This spiritual message needs to be at the core of all aspects of treatment.

It has been my experience that although many treatment centers believe the above and indeed print in their brochures a loving self-acceptance as the goal of treatment, still the language used and ideas conveyed are suspiciously religious in inference. Often their themes for meditation and prayer are exclusively Biblical:

a) Moses escaping slavery in Egypt
b) Cain and Abel — depicting jealousy
c) David and Goliath — overcoming incredible odds

In the New Testament:

a) Jesus being tempted in the desert
b) The Sermon on the Mount
c) The miracles of healing

d) The prodigal son
e) Jesus dying that we might live
f) The "new life" of the Resurrection

The Lord's Prayer often is used as the prayer for recovery, unconsciously disregarding the fact that many people in treatment are Jewish, agnostic, atheist or from other religions.

Words are used in prayer and meditation exercises that are specifically religious and cannot be understood without a knowledge of Judeo-Christian theology. Examples:

grace	soul
redemption	confession
sin	testimony
absolution	Savior
discipleship	remnant

I am not suggesting that the above cannot have an important role to play in the discovering and nurturing of the spiritual life, but the words and phrases need explaining; more specifically, they need to be understood within the context of a recovery program. Also, scriptural stories and references need to be supplemented with secular spiritual words and stories that are less offensive and scary to many people, clearly making the point that our Spirituality is not dependent on being religious!

Suggested words and themes:

joy	acceptance	freedom
love	power	energy
forgiveness	surrender	communication
light	serenity	hugs
courage	peace	openness
honesty	gratitude	hope

If we understand the challenge of Spirituality as being the discovery of God in His or Her world, in meaningful relationships, in the living of our lives, then we need to communicate a similar message in treatment.

Alongside the Lord's Prayer, let us encourage patients to write and create prayers and meditations that are meaningful to them, using their words and expressions to convey *the God of their understanding,* developing themes that they consider to be important.

Alongside Gospel ballads, let us hear the popular songs of today's generation that express the spiritual themes of
> change,
>> love,
>>> forgiveness
>>>> and acceptance.

Let dance, music, art, poetry, literature, movies, discussion and outside activities be used in presenting the concept of the "Big God". Only when we encounter the challenge and adventure of life, life in its fullness, can the spiritual awakening be activated.

Because every aspect of healing is spiritual, we need to present the challenge of a recovering lifestyle in treatment. Some years ago, a French priest tried to revolutionize prayer and meditation by writing about aspects of life that normally are not associated with God and spirituality. His subjects included The Brick, Posters, The Tractor, Prayer Before a Five-pound Note, The Wire Fence and this one, called *The Pornographic Magazine:*

The office workers all contributed to buy it.
The boy ran to fetch it.
And pored over it on the way back.
Here it is.
On its shining pages, naked bodies are exposed,
Going from office to office, from hand to hand;
Such foolish giggles, such lustful glances . . .
Empty bodies, soulless, bodies,
Adult toys for the hardened and the soiled.

And yet, Lord, man's body is beautiful.
From the beginning, you, the supreme Artist, held the
*   model before you, knowing that one day you would*
*   dwell in a human body when taking on the nature of*
*   man.*
Slowly you shaped it with your powerful hands; and into
*   its inert matter you breathed a living soul.*
From then on, Lord, you asked us to respect the body,
*   for the whole body is a conveyor of the spirit,*
And we need this sensitive instrument that our spirits
*   may commune with those of our brothers.*

Michel Quoist, *Prayer of Life*

Those of us who work and teach in treatment centers need to be searching for new and exciting ways of talking about God and developing Spirituality in our lives. A sentence in Michel Quoist's meditation — ". . . you asked us to respect the body, for the whole body is a conveyor of the spirit . . ." — holds the key to discovering a comprehensive approach to Spirituality in treatment. Remember, spirituality concerns the healing of the whole body. God does not make junk. The body, mind and emotions all proclaim the God-given divinity of mankind; Spirituality concerns the whole man.

The tragedy in describing the human being as body, mind and spirit is that it specifically separates the spirit (spirituality) from the activities that concern the body and mind. This has subconsciously predisposed people to think that Spirituality involves prayer and meditation, but they tend not to connect spirituality with nutrition, sexuality, science, feelings, jogging or that healing activity called "hugging". And this is a great mistake. Spirituality embraces the work of the doctor, nurse, physiotherapist, counselor, dietitian, cook and visiting clergyperson who might conduct the spirituality lecture. Once this concept is understood in the treatment center and explained enthusiastically to patients, families and employers, the miracle of recovery can comprehensively begin.

This diagram explains the concept:

Emotions/Feelings

Body/Physical   Mental/Mind

Anger
Loneliness
Fear
Confusion
Love
Acceptance
Joy

Organ dysfunction
Nutrition
Exercise
Sleep
Hugs
Sexuality

Choices
Dreams
Hopes
Ideas
Suggestions
Criticism

It is important that we consistently connect and explain this concept of Spirituality to all aspects of treatment and recovery.

The awareness of our dysfunctional behavior creates the possibility for discovering our spiritual values. If we believe that in confronting what is sick and unhealthy, we are able to apprehend what needs to be done for recovery — developing the idea that in the acceptance of this disease are the seeds of wellness — then the miracle of treatment is realized. Spirituality is knowing that we have the power to change.

Spirituality is discovering that negatives can be turned into positives. Spirituality involves the miracle of creative effort. I have provocatively suggested throughout this book that it is the disease that guides us into wellness; knowing what is wrong is the precondition for doing what is right; we can only turn in a new direction what we have apprehended. Spiritual power emerges in the acceptance of our imperfections.

Let us put this idea to the test.

Disease process (escape)	*Spiritual values (reality)*
1. Unintelligible God	1. God as we understand Him/Her
2. Denial	2. Admittance/acceptance
3. Dishonesty	3. Honesty
4. Apathy/pessimism	4. Energy/enthusiasm
5. Anger	5. Peace/serenity
6. Manipulation	6. Straightforwardness
7. Physical sickness	7. Health
8. Isolation	8. Involvement
9. Depression	9. Hope
10. Guilt/shame	10. Forgiveness/freedom
11. Boredom	11. Joy in living
12. Fear	12. Self-confidence/esteem

I believe that the life of Jesus Christ and all the great religious and spiritual leaders revealed these spiritual values. When Jesus said, "I came that you might have life and have it abundantly," (St. John, 10:10). He was talking about realizing and expressing our yes to life. Treatment involves the development of these spiritual values that can be experienced and expressed in our recovering lives. We have discovered the power to become positive and creative human beings.

In my book *Say Yes To Life . . . Daily Meditations for Recovery*, I describe the spiritual lifestyle in this way:

Some things I seem to know intuitively: and I know that Spirituality is involved in and affects everything. In a human being, it combines the physical, mental and emotional, but it also reaches beyond the human being and connects the peoples of the world. Spirituality is the force for good and wholeness in this universe.

This is not just an opinion or thought. It is a feeling that runs so deep in my being that I know it must be true. When I read, hear music or see movies, this feeling is often evoked, and I know God is alive in His world and wanting it to be ONE.

And this is what treatment is about.

ABOUT THE AUTHOR

Father Leo Booth is Addiction Consultant to Presbyterian Intercommunity Hospital's Chemical Dependency Center, Whittier, California. He is a native of England and was educated at King's College and St. Augustine's. For a short time he tutored the Chaplain's course at Christ College, Cambridge, on the subject of "Spirituality and Addiction". He has degrees in divinity and philosophy and is a Certified Alcoholism Counselor as well as a Certified Eating Disorders Counselor.

Father Leo had a personal "moment" in 1977, following an automobile accident when he recognized that he was an alcoholic. Following treatment at Warlingham Park Hospital in Sussex, England, he began to devote his energies helping other alcoholics and their families by his own methods of recognizing the "giveness" of Spirituality. He defines Spirituality as: "that which enables the development of creative and positive attitudes in all areas of life." Father Leo believes vulnerability to be the key to the God-given power of choice, "bleeding in order to heal". Spirituality is perceiving the miracle that is within.

Father Leo speaks Internationally at Drug Conferences, universities and industrial groups. In 1983 he was made Spiritual Advisor to the Dangerous Drug Board, Quezon City, Manila, and has been involved in developing an education program based on "Spirituality and Recovery" for the recovering Filipinos. He has also visited and advised the Government Drug Agency in Thailand.

Father Leo has appeared on "The Oprah Winfrey Show", "Hour Magazine" and "The Today Show" as well as numerous radio programs to discuss aspects of Spirituality and Recovery. He also contributes to "Professional Counselor Magazine".

He has written the following books: *Spirituality and Recovery . . . A Guide to Positive Living, Meditations For Compulsive People* and *Say Yes to Life . . . Daily Meditations.*

Since arriving in America in 1981 Father Leo has received the following appointments: Board of Directors, National Council on Alcoholism, Los Angeles; Board Member, Jellinek Medical Association; International Association of Eating Disorders Professional, Advisory Board; and Associate Priest, St. Mark's Episcopal Church, Downey, California 90241.

Other Books By . . .

HEALTH COMMUNICATIONS, INC.

Enterprise Center
3201 Southwest 15th Street
Deerifield Beach, FL 33442
Phone: 800-851-9100

ADULT CHILDREN OF ALCOHOLICS
Janet Woititz
Over a year on The New York Times Best Seller list,this book is the primer
on Adult Children of Alcoholics.
ISBN 0-932194-15-X   **$6.95**

STRUGGLE FOR INTIMACY
Janet Woititz
Another best seller, this book gives insightful advice on learning to love
more fully.
ISBN 0-932194-25-7   **$6.95**

DAILY AFFIRMATIONS: For Adult Children of Alcoholics
Rokelle Lerner
These positive affirmations for every day of the year paint a mental picture
of your life as you choose it to be.
ISBN 0-932194-27-3   **$6.95**

*CHOICEMAKING: For Co-dependents, Adult Children and Spirituality
Seekers* — Sharon Wegscheider-Cruse
This useful book defines the problems and solves them in a positive way.
ISBN 0-932194-26-5   **$9.95**

LEARNING TO LOVE YOURSELF: Finding Your Self-Worth
Sharon Wegscheider-Cruse
"Self-worth is a choice, not a birthright", says the author as she shows us
how we can choose positive self-esteem.
ISBN 0-932194-39-7   **$7.95**

LET GO AND GROW: Recovery for Adult Children
Robert Ackerman
An in-depth study of the different characteristics of adult children of
alcoholics with guidelines for recovery.
ISBN 0-932194-51-6   **$8.95**

LOST IN THE SHUFFLE: The Co-dependent Reality
Robert Subby
A look at the unreal rules the co-dependent lives by and the way out of the
dis-eased reality.
ISBN 0-932194-45-1   **$8.95**

New Books . . .
from Health Communications

BRADSHAW ON: THE FAMILY: A Revolutionary Way of Self-Discovery
John Bradshaw
The host of the nationally televised series of the same name shows us how families can be healed and we as individuals can realize our full potential.
ISBN 0-932194-54-0   **$9.95**

HEALING THE CHILD WITHIN: Discovery and Recovery for Adult Children of Dysfunctional Families — Charles Whitfield
Dr. Whitfield defines, describes and discovers how we can reach our Child Within to heal and nurture our woundedness.
ISBN 0-932194-40-0   **$8.95**

WHISKY'S SONG: An Explicit Story of Surviving in an Alcoholic Home
Mitzi Chandler
A beautiful but brutal story of growing up where violence and neglect are everyday occurrences conveys a positive message of survival and love.
ISBN 0-932194-42-7   **$6.95**

New Books on Spiritual Recovery . . .
from Health Communications

THE JOURNEY WITHIN: A Spiritual Path to Recovery
Ruth Fishel
This book will lead you from your dysfunctional beginnings to the place within where renewal occurs.
ISBN 0-932194-41-9   **$8.95**

LEARNING TO LIVE IN THE NOW: 6-Week Personal Plan To Recovery
Ruth Fishel
The author gently introduces you to the valuable healing tools of meditation, positive creative visualization and affirmations.
ISBN 0-932194-62-1   **$7.95**

GENESIS: Spirituality in Recovery for Co-dependents
by Julie D. Bowden and Herbert L. Gravitz
A self-help spiritual program for adult children of trauma, an in-depth look at "turning it over" and "letting go".
ISBN 0-932194-56-7   **$6.95**

GIFTS FOR PERSONAL GROWTH AND RECOVERY
Wayne Kritsberg
Gifts for healing which include journal writing, breathing, positioning and meditation.
ISBN 0-932194-60-5   **$6.95**

Books from . . .
Health Communications

THIRTY-TWO ELEPHANT REMINDERS: A Book of Healthy Rules
Mary M. McKee
Concise advice by 32 wise elephants whose wit and good humor will also be appearing in a 12-step calendar and greeting cards.
ISBN 0-932194-59-1   **$3.95**

BREAKING THE CYCLE OF ADDICTION: For Adult Children of Alcoholics
Patricia O'Gorman and Philip Oliver-Diaz
For parents who were raised in addicted families, this guide teaches you about Breaking the Cycle of Addiction from *your* parents to your children. Must reading for any parent.
ISBN 0-932194-37-0   **$8.95**

AFTER THE TEARS: Reclaiming The Personal Losses of Childhood
Jane Middelton-Moz and Lorie Dwinnel
Your lost childhood must be grieved in order for you to recapture your self-worth and enjoyment of life. This book will show you how.
ISBN 0-932194-36-2   **$7.95**

ADULT CHILDREN OF ALCOHOLICS SYNDROME: From Discovery to Recovery
Wayne Kritsberg
Through the Family Integration System and foundations for healing the wounds of an alcoholic-influenced childhood are laid in this important book.
ISBN 0-932194-30-3   **$7.95**

OTHERWISE PERFECT: People and Their Problems with Weight
Mary S. Stuart and Lynnzy Orr
This book deals with all the varieties of eating disorders, from anorexia to obesity, and how to cope sensibly and successfully.
ISBN 0-932194-57-5   **$7.95**

Orders must be prepaid by check, money order, MasterCard or Visa. Purchase orders from agencies accepted (attach P.O. documentation) for billing. Net 30 days.

Minimum shipping/handling — $1.25 for orders less than $25. For orders over $25, add 5% of total for shipping and handling. Florida residents add 5% sales tax.

MOVE AHEAD IN YOUR RECOVERY!

With Changes Magazine — America's Leading Recovery Publication

Receive A Free Issue Now!

Changes Magazine gives you the vital self-healing tools you need to understand your inner self and reach your personal recovery potential.

Each copy of **Changes** brings you new information on today's recovery issues like self-esteem, intimacy, codependency, and the inner child. Plus you'll receive news on support groups, innovative recovery techniques, and insights from featured personalities like Oprah Winfrey, John Bradshaw, and Leo Buscaglia.

Discover the magazine that's helping thousands of people across the United States develop inner peace and personal satisfaction.

TAKE THIS SPECIAL OPPORTUNITY TO RECEIVE A FREE ISSUE OF CHANGES
BY RETURNING THE COUPON BELOW.

Yes, please send me my free issue of **Changes** Magazine — a $3.75 newsstand value! If I decide to subscribe, I'll pay your invoice for $18.00 for a one-year subscription (6 issues including my complimentary issue) and save 20% off the newsstand price. If I don't choose to subscribe, I'll simply write "Cancel" on the invoice, return it to you, and owe nothing.

Name _____
(please print)

Address _____ Apt. _____

City _____ State _____ Zip_____
FCCHG2

☐ Please add my name to your mailing list for advance notice of conferences in my area plus catalogs of recovery books, audio tapes, and special gifts.

SEND TO: The U.S. Journal Inc./Subscriptions
3201 SW 15th St.
Deerfield Beach, FL 33442-8190